SEED to SUPPER

MICHELLE DARMODY
ILLUSTRATED BY RUTH GRAHAM

THE JOURNEY OF YOUR FOOD
FROM THE GROUND UP

Nine Bean Rows

23 Mountjoy Square

Dublin

D01 E0F8

Ireland

@9beanrowsbooks

ninebeanrowsbooks.com

First published 2024

Text © Michelle Darmody, 2024

Illustrations © Ruth Graham, 2024

ISBN: 978-1-7392105-7-1

Editor: Kristin Jensen

Illustration: Ruth Graham ruthgraham.ie

Design and layout: EMC Design Ltd emcdesign.org.uk

Indexer: Jane Rogers

Printed by L&C Printing Group, Poland

The paper in this book is produced using pulp from managed forests.

All rights reserved.

No part of this publication may be copied, reproduced or transmitted in any form or by any means without written permission of the publishers.

A CIP catalogue record for this book is available from the British Library.

10 9 8 7 6 5 4 3 2 1

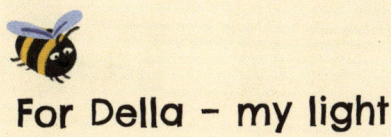
For Della – my light

CONTENTS

01 Seeds page 6

02 Soil page 14

03 Pollinating page 24

04 Growing page 32

05 Picking page 44

06 Tasting page 52

07 Buying page 60

08 Cooking page 70

09 Reusing page 106

10 Eating page 120

INTRODUCTION

I love food. I love eating it, cooking it, learning about how it grows and seeing where it comes from. When I visit another country, the first thing I want to do is go to a café or a small local restaurant to see how people eat together.

I have put this love into writing this book. It tells the story of how most of our food starts as a seed, then follows the journey of the seed through the soil, into our kitchens and onto our plates.

It's full of bits of information that will help you in the garden, in the kitchen or around a table. If you don't have space to grow food or somewhere to cook, there are lots of other make-and-do activities.

As well as tips about when to grow herbs, fruit and vegetables and diagrams to help you grate, crush and chop, this book also encourages you to pay attention to how food is sold through advertising. This is important to talk about when you are young, as there can be a lot of pressure to buy certain foods.

The book also talks about how food connects people, no matter what part of the world they come from, and looks at ways people eat around the world. Even though there might be slight differences, we all share traditions around food. A simple recipe or even a fruit or vegetable can connect you with someone on the other side of the world, because the tomato crossed the globe as a seed hundreds of years ago and made its home in new countries and influenced how people in those new countries cook and eat.

I hope you enjoy reading, exploring and cooking from this book as much as I enjoyed writing it. Let's go on the journey together from seed to supper to learn how a bee's waggle and a worm's wiggle help to feed the world.

SEEDS

Food starts with a seed

There are thousands of different types of seeds that grow into food, but we grow only a small number of them on farms. Usually the seeds that are used have been chosen for a reason. They might grow into a tree that has juicy fruit, like an orange, or perhaps the seeds or fruit are easy to transport to other countries, like bananas with their thick skins. Or the plant might have a superpower that makes it impossible for bugs or insects to eat it.

Seeds come in all shapes and sizes

Seeds come in all different sizes and also in some very strange shapes. Each seed has adapted to help it grow best. A pip in an orange and a stone in a peach are both seeds. So are the tiny, almost invisible seeds that grow into heads of lettuce. A sea coconut palm has the largest and heaviest seeds on earth. They can be half a metre long and weigh as much as a big penguin!

How seeds move from place to place

In the summer you might see fluffy white dandelion seeds floating through the air or 'helicopters' from a sycamore tree swirling to the ground in autumn. The wind carries these seeds so that they can find space to grow, away from the shadow of their parent plant.

Animals can also carry seeds, as some seeds have little tentacles that stick to their fur. Other seeds come out in their poo after the animal eats them. Plants from really hot parts of the world have clever ways of spreading their seeds: the seed pods only open if there is a forest fire and lots of smoke.

Some seeds are in pods that burst open in a dramatic way, spreading the seeds as far as they can. When their pods pop, the seeds of a witch hazel tree can fly through the air for nearly **10 metres** – that's the length of a double-decker bus. Peas and beans also spread their seeds this way. Their pods will explode open if they are left to dry out on the plant – that is, if we don't pick them and eat them first!

Confused vegetables

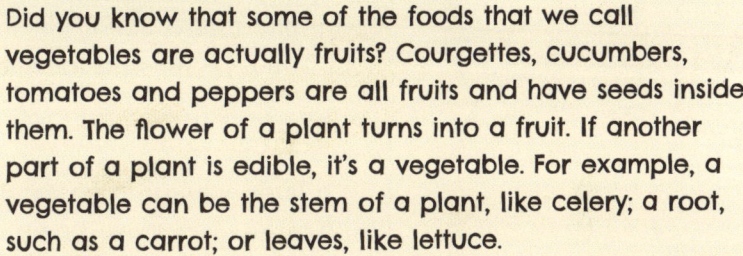

Did you know that some of the foods that we call vegetables are actually fruits? Courgettes, cucumbers, tomatoes and peppers are all fruits and have seeds inside them. The flower of a plant turns into a fruit. If another part of a plant is edible, it's a vegetable. For example, a vegetable can be the stem of a plant, like celery; a root, such as a carrot; or leaves, like lettuce.

A fruit's job is to cover and protect the seeds. Not all fruits contain the same number of seeds. Tomatoes, cucumbers, peppers and melons usually have lots of seeds. Oranges, apples and pears contain about 10 seeds in each fruit.

Eating seeds

People plant seeds that will grow into different types of plants because they will provide energy or because people like how they taste. Grains of wheat, which are used to make bread, and oats, which are used to make porridge, are varieties of seeds. Other seeds can be eaten without cooking them, like sesame seeds, sunflower seeds and chia seeds.

Legumes, such as peas and beans, are also seeds. So are nuts. Peanuts are not actually nuts, but a type of legume. They grow under the ground, not on trees.

Seeds even help us to cook our food by providing us with cooking oils.

Biodiversity

Using the same seeds all the time can lead to biodiversity loss. Biodiversity means there is a wide variety of different plants growing in an area, which helps different animals and insects to live there. Biodiversity loss happens when plants that used to live in the area don't get a chance to grow. This means they begin to disappear, which makes life harder for animals, birds and other creatures.

Seed banks

Seed banks are places around the world where a huge variety of seeds are stored in case we ever need them for food in the future. Seed banks can also be used to learn more about plants and for scientific research.

The seed banks are inside well-protected buildings. One is buried inside an icy mountain in the Arctic Circle. Another is in a huge vault in a desert. The buildings are so strong that they would survive being hit by an earthquake or being flooded.

A carrot has around **32,000** genes, which is about **20%** more than a human has.

Genes

Genes are inside all living things. Genes are patterns, or instructions, that tell things how to grow. It is how these genes are combined in your body (or in a plant) that makes us all different.

For example, your genes tell your body to make your eyes blue or your hair black. In a plant, genes tell it to become a red tomato or an orange carrot. Two rice plants with a different mix of genes will grow differently. One might grow very quickly and have big grains of rice ready for the farmer to harvest, but another with a different mix of genes could take much longer to grow and have smaller grains.

Changing genes

Genes can be changed to make plants grow in different ways. Some seeds have been changed by scientists. They do this by modifying or editing a plant's genes in a laboratory. For instance, the genes in some potatoes have been changed to make the potatoes less tasty for bugs or insects. This is called genetic modification and foods that are modified in this way are called GMO foods.

Some people think GMO foods are good because it can make plants easier to grow. Others don't like GMO foods as they think they are bad for the environment and bad for people. It also means farmers have to pay a higher price for the seeds from the scientists who modified them.

There is a newer way that scientists can change foods, called genetic editing. It uses the genes that are already in the plant instead of mixing them with genes from something else.

Seeds in space

In the International Space Station, astronauts plant seeds in water so that they can grow fresh food to eat. This way of growing is called hydroponics and it's used here on Earth too. The seeds are sprinkled onto a special mat and kept warm under bright lights. Astronauts have grown chillies in their space station. They had a spicy taco dinner to celebrate picking them! Growing fresh food helps keep the astronauts healthy. Bringing seeds into space will be even more important when space missions get longer and astronauts travel further into the galaxy.

HOW SEEDS GROW

All the information that a seed needs to grow into a plant is hidden inside it. The outer part of the seed, called a seed coat, protects this information.

Some seed coats are sticky, some are fuzzy, some are prickly and some are very hard.

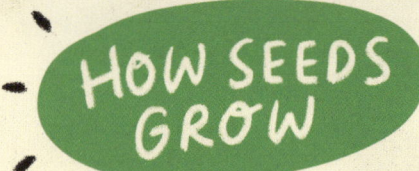

All seeds store food inside them. They feed on this food until they stretch out their first leaves. Once the seed has produced leaves, it's called a seedling and it gets its energy from the sun. It will also start to take nutrients from the soil. Nutrients are chemicals used by all living things to help them grow.

FROM SEED TO PLANT

Seeds are resting inside their coats, waiting to grow. The seed coat cracks open once the growing process starts. All seeds, no matter what shape or size, need three things to kickstart their growth: water, oxygen and the perfect temperature. Seeds can wait a long time for the conditions to be just right.

Activity: Saving seeds

You will need:
- Peas, beans and/or tomatoes that you have grown
- Saucers
- Paper envelopes
- Glass jars with tight-fitting lids

If a fruit or vegetable grew well for you one year, saving the seeds means you can grow it again the next year. Saving seeds also saves money, as you won't have to buy more packets of seeds.

Seeds are all different, so there are different ways of saving them. One good rule for all seeds is to keep them cool and dry over the winter while you wait to plant them in the spring.

How to save peas and beans

1 Take the fat little peas or beans out of their pods towards the end of the summer. Put them on a saucer and dry them out on a windowsill.

2 Once they are completely dry, put the peas or beans in a paper envelope, then put the envelope in a clean glass jar with a tight-fitting lid. Keep the jar in cool, dry place until spring.

How to save tomato seeds

1 Cut a good, healthy-looking tomato in half and squeeze out the seeds. They will be sticky from the jelly-like flesh that is attached to them.

2 Put the seeds in a saucer of water. Leave it on a windowsill for a few days, until the bits of tomato get mouldy.

3 Wash the seeds in a big bowl of water – the ones that sink to the bottom of the bowl are the best ones to dry out and keep. Make sure all the jelly is washed off the seeds.

4 Put the seeds on a clean, dry saucer and leave them on your windowsill for a few days, until they have completely dried out.

5 Put the seeds in a paper envelope, then put the envelope in a clean glass jar with a tight-fitting lid. Keep the jar in a cool, dry place until spring.

Activity: Grow a seedling

You will need:
- Eggshells and an egg carton (or small pots or cardboard tubes)
- Soil or compost
- Seeds
- Stones
- Waterproof paint
- Paintbrush

Peas and beans are a good choice when you are starting to grow your own food because they push up through the soil with lots of energy. You can see them grow into a baby plant quite quickly.

> Your plants will face a few dangers once they are outdoors, such as wind and rain, but mainly insects looking for a snack. It's a good idea to plant a lot of seeds because some will be lost to these dangers.

How to start growing your seedling

1. Eggshells are ideal for planting seeds. (You can use small pots or the cardboard tube inside of a toilet roll if you don't have empty eggshells.) Crack your egg near the top so you have a nice deep shell to fill with soil or compost. (Don't forget to use the egg in a tasty breakfast, lunch or dinner!) Clean the shell to remove any sticky film from the inside, then gently fill it with compost or soil.

2. Make a hole in the soil with your finger to the correct depth for your seed. A good rule is to plant a seed about the same distance below the surface as the size of the seed. For example, a big avocado stone needs to be much deeper in the soil than the small seed of a tomato plant or a pea.

3. Put your seed inside the hole, then cover it over with soil. Gently pat down, then water your eggshell. Put it into an empty egg carton and choose a nice bright spot on a windowsill for it to sit.

4. Check it each day and water it when it's drying out. You should see a green stalk starting to push its way up through the soil.

5. Your seedling will grow towards the sunshine. Turn the seedling around every day so it doesn't get spindly, which means it gets too long and skinny and can't hold its head up high.

6. Once the second bunch of leaves have pushed out from the stem of the seedling, replant it outside in the garden or in a bigger pot for the windowsill.

7. When it's time to replant, gently make a few cracks in the eggshell by tapping it on the top of a table, then pop the shell, seedling and all, into the soil. The eggshell will disappear into the soil and give it some extra calcium. Calcium helps humans to grow and it helps plants to become strong too.

8. It's easy to forget what seeds you planted and seedlings can all look alike. Paint a picture of the plant you are growing on a stone and put it beside your eggshells or pots. Use waterproof paint if you want to put your stones outside with your seedlings.

> If you're planting different things, read the back of the seed packets to see what that seed likes. Different seeds like different temperatures or different amounts of sunlight. Lettuce seeds, for example, like lots of light to germinate. When planting them, just scatter them over the soil instead of pushing them into it.

SOIL

What is soil?

There is a mysterious world of soil beneath our feet. You might just see it as dirt or mud to squelch with your wellies, but soil is special.

Soil is also complicated. It's made up of lots of different things, such as minerals, water, air and old bits of plants and trees. It's also full of creatures like worms and beetles wriggling and crawling about.

Most plants use roots to hold on tightly to the soil, and the soil helps these plants to grow. Their roots soak up water and help the plants to get the food they need from the soil.

There is no soil on Mars or on the moon, which is one of the reasons that plants don't grow there.

Soil is sometimes called earth, which is a nice name for it, as it's an important part of the planet Earth that we live on. Soil is the thin layer that covers about 10% of our planet's surface.

Types of soil

Soil is different from one country to another. It can even be different from one field to another! Some plants like the sandy soil that forms near the ocean, while others love the deep, brown, wet soil that forms near a bog or at a river's edge.

There are six different types of soil: clay, silt, sandy soil, chalky soil, loam and peat soil.

CLAY
SILT

SANDY

CHALKY

LOAM

PEAT

How soil is made

All soil is made really, **really** slowly through the weathering and erosion of rocks. This happens over a long period of time when the rock is broken up by weather or water. The rock first breaks into chunks, then these chunks break down into smaller pieces that make up soil.

Soil is also made from old plants piling up on top of each other. In most parts of the world, soil takes thousands of years to form. Soil can form a bit quicker in hot, damp places, but it still takes a long time.

The oldest soil on Earth is in South Africa, where it is thought to be 3 BILLION years old.

Soil horizons

If you see a section of soil that has been cut into, like on a building site, you might be able to see lots of layers of different colours and textures. These are called soil horizons. They show us how different types of soil were made over time. The different colours were made at different stages, often in different centuries.

The top layer of soil is the best for growing vegetables and crops. This layer has the most minerals and food that help plants to grow.

Soil makes you smile

Putting your hands in soil or digging in a garden can be good for you. Soil contains bacteria that help to make your brain happier and keep you smiling.

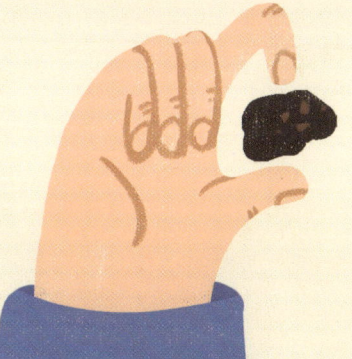

Soil is full of life

The soil is busy with creatures crawling about, making their homes, finding something to eat or creating a nice cosy spot to lay their eggs. It's home to worms, insects, centipedes, mushrooms, moles, grubs and lots of different types of bacteria.

You can see some of the things that live in the soil, but others, like bacteria, are so tiny that you need a powerful microscope to see them.

One teaspoon of soil can contain **1 BILLION** bacteria. That means just 8 teaspoons of soil have more bacteria inside them than the number of people on Earth!

Worms take care of the soil

It's a good sign if you find lots of worms in your vegetable patch or garden. When earthworms wriggle their way through the soil, the tunnels and holes that they make help air get into the soil. They also help to break up big lumps of soil. The worms are pretty much eating the soil and pooping it back out, making it better for growing as they go.

Root vegetables like carrots or parsnips especially enjoy it when there are lots of worms in the soil because it makes it much easier for them to push their way down and form nice juicy roots that we can pick and eat.

Who works with soil?

Soil is an important part of many people's jobs. Archaeologists, some scientists and foresters (people who plant and care for trees) all work with soil. Because we build our buildings on top of soil, it's also important for builders and construction workers.

Soil is probably most important for farmers because healthy soil helps to make our food. In fact, soil is important for 95% of all the food that's produced in the world. (See page 20 to learn about food that doesn't need soil to grow.)

Making medicine from soil

When people are sick, doctors sometimes give them antibiotics to help them get better. Almost all the antibiotics that we use come from little organisms and bacteria in the soil!

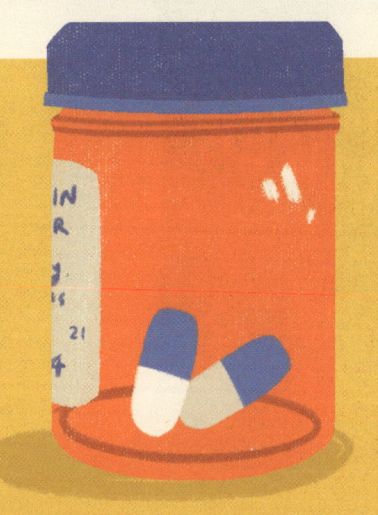

Worms have no arms and legs, but did you know they have no eyes or ears either? They can sense vibrations and light through their skin. They can also travel backwards and forwards and can move a rock that is **60 times** their own weight!

Soakage

Soil soaks up water, which helps to stop flooding. When the roots of a plant grow under the soil, they help the land by stopping erosion. This is because the roots cause the soil and stones to stick together.

Soil also drains water, which helps to clean it. People then clean water even more to make it safe to drink.

Improving soil

When plants and vegetables grow in soil, they soak up lots of nutrients to help them grow. This means the soil might not be as good for growing food the next year because there are fewer nutrients for the plants to feed on. Farmers and growers can improve the soil by adding nutrients or by rotating crops that soak up different minerals and food each year.

More peas, please!

Certain plants put some of their food back into the soil. Peas and beans do this. So does clover, the little purple-flowered plant that grows wild. Plant clover in your vegetable patch at the end of the summer. It will grow there all winter and add richness to the soil for the following spring.

Clover helps to reduce the amount of chemical fertilizers going onto a field because it's a good natural fertilizer that puts nitrogen back into the soil.

Fertilizers

Fertilizer that is made in factories has helped us grow enough food to feed the world, but using these fertilizers can cause problems in lakes and rivers. Seaweed, chicken poo and fallen leaves are all natural fertilizers. Some clever people are also using food waste to make fertilizer.

An invention for making fertilizer called the Haber-Bosch process helped the population on Earth grow from **1 billion** people to over **7.5 billion** people today. This invention made fertilizer available to farmers all over the world. Once farmers could use it, they were able to grow lots of food to feed more and more people.

Farming with soil

Farmers use soil in many ways to grow food. Some have huge fields and use machines to plough the fields. Very big farms that use big machines are called intensive farms. This intensive farming has helped to grow a lot of food, but it can also damage the soil because more fertilizer is used and the same crop is planted over large spaces.

Other farmers don't dig the soil at all, as they want to keep all the minerals and bacteria inside it. This is called regenerative farming.

In some parts of the world, farmers only grow enough food for themselves and just a few other people in their neighbourhoods. On bigger intensive farms, the farmer sells what they grow. The food is sent around the world on ships and brought to the shops. Or it can be used to make food in factories. For example, breakfast cereals are made in factories from farmed crops such as corn or wheat.

Growing plants without soil

Most plants need soil to survive, but a few unusual ones grow in different ways. Some plants can dig their roots into tiny cracks in rocks. They get enough food to grow from the air around them and from minerals in the rock. Other plants can grow on tree branches. These types of plants are called epiphytes. Most orchids and some ferns grow this way.

Magic spring onions

Some vegetables can start to regrow without soil. If you have a bunch of spring onions, save the white ends that have small roots sticking out of them. Put them in a glass of water and put the glass on a windowsill. They will grow back in a few weeks. This is because they are getting minerals from the water.

Wood Wide Web

Trees use the soil, their roots and tiny threads of mushrooms, called mycelium, to communicate or 'talk' with each other. This is sometimes called the Wood Wide Web. The mushrooms and roots spread through the soil in a forest and connect the trees together. The trees can talk about what food they are getting from the soil. They can also help each other by sending a warning if they sense something that might harm another tree, like a pest or disease.

Activity: Framing nature

You will need:
- 4 nice straight twigs
- Ruler or measuring tape
- Some twine or wool
- Or use an old picture frame instead of the twigs and twine or wool
- Colouring pencils
- Your activity notebook or a piece of paper

You can use a small notebook to write down all the information from this activity and then use it for other activities in the book too.

1. Using four nice straight twigs, try to make a frame about 30cm square. Use a ruler or measuring tape to get the size right, but don't worry if it's a bit bigger or smaller. Tie each of the four corners together with twine or wool.

Scientists use a square frame like this for studying ecology and geography or for examining the biodiversity in an area. They call it a quadrat.

2. Pick a place in your garden or in a local park to do your investigation with the frame. Bring some colouring pencils and your activity notebook or a piece of paper with you. The frame might be delicate, so be careful with it.

3. Put the frame on the ground wherever you choose. Take a close look at everything that is inside your frame and at the type of soil that is on the ground. There might be lots of tiny bugs, different kinds of grasses or flowers, bits of leaves or parts of larger plants. Or there could be some snails, shells or stones. Can you see different colours, textures or patterns? You might be surprised at how many things you find inside your frame!

4. Draw everything you see or make separate drawings of different leaves, shells, stones, snails or insects. Imagine what it would be like to be their size, living among skyscrapers of grass and flowers.

5. Now try a different area – perhaps nearby or even somewhere completely different, or investigate at another time of day. Note what is different or what is the same.

Activity: Test your soil

You will need:
- Soil samples
- Bread soda
- Distilled white vinegar
- Tablespoon and teaspoon
- Small bowl
- Measuring jug
- Small cup
- Kitchen scale
- Small baking tray

Different plants like different types of soil, so testing your soil will help you get the most from your vegetable patch. After you do your tests, you can change the soil by adding compost, using mulch or adding sand.

What is pH?

pH measures how acidic or alkaline something is on a scale from 1 to 14. It's important to know the pH of your soil because plants are a bit fussy about what pH they like. Carrots, peppers and tomatoes like soil that is acidic. Kale, beans and beetroot like alkaline soil.

If the pH number is low, it means there is a lot of acid in the soil. If it's high, it means there is a lot of alkaline. Too much of either stops the plants absorbing nutrients from the soil.

Test how much water is in the soil

1. Get a small cup of soil. Make sure there are no worms or bugs in it before you start your experiment.
2. Weigh the soil with a kitchen scale and write down its weight.
3. Spread the soil on a small baking tray and pop it on a sunny windowsill. Leave it for a day or two, until it's nice and dry.
4. Weigh it again in the same cup that you weighed it in before. The difference in weight shows the amount of water that came out of the soil as it dried in the sun.

Test the soil texture

Some plants, such as herbs like rosemary and thyme, love sandy soil. Other plants, like vegetables such as spinach and cauliflower, love damp soil that is full of clay and holds the water inside.

1. Test the texture of soil by squeezing some moist (but not too wet) soil in the palm of your hand. If it holds its shape, it's sticky soil with a lot of clay. If it falls apart in your hand, it's grainy, sandy soil that water can run through easily.

How to test soil pH

You can get a soil testing kit in a shop that will tell you what pH your soil is, but you also can test soil without a pH kit. To test if soil is acidic, you will need bread soda. To test if it is alkaline, use vinegar.

1. To see if soil is acidic, put 2 tablespoons of soil in a bowl and mix it with 1 tablespoon of water. Add 1 teaspoon of bread soda and watch to see if the soil fizzes. If it does, it means the soil is acidic because a chemical reaction is happening with the bread soda and the acid in the soil.
2. To see if soil is alkaline, pour 125ml of distilled white vinegar in a bowl and add 2 tablespoons of soil. Watch to see if the soil fizzes in the vinegar. If it does, it means the soil is alkaline because a chemical reaction is happening with the vinegar and the alkali in the soil.

POLLINATING

What is pollination?

Flowers produce a powdery substance called pollen that helps them to reproduce and make more flowers and seeds the next year. The pollen needs to be spread from one flower to another so that plants can reproduce – this is called pollination.

The wind can help with pollination, but most of our food crops, wildflowers and trees need creatures and insects to do this work. When they spread the pollen from flower to flower, most creatures get nectar in return (nectar is a sweet liquid made by the flowers).

Bees are the most famous pollinators, but lots of other creatures help with this important task.

POLLEN

How pollinators help plants grow

Our food cycle relies on pollination because fruit and vegetables start out as flowers.

A pollinator wiggles its way into the centre of a flower to drink the nectar. While it's doing this, tiny grains of pollen stick to its body and hairy legs.

When the pollinator moves to the next flower, it takes the pollen with it to pollinate that flower.

After pollination, the petals fall off the flower. The centre swells up to make a fruit with the seeds of the plant tucked safely inside.

This fruit grows under the warm sun and gets sweeter and juicier until it's picked or falls off the plant.

The BEE'S KNEES

Shapes, smells and colours that attract pollinators

Pollinators all have differently shaped mouths, so they like different types of plants. Certain flower shapes are easy for one type of pollinator to feed on but not another.

Smells, shapes and colours all attract hungry pollinators. Beetles like spicy scented flowers, while hoverflies like sweet-smelling flowers.

Purple, blue and violet are bees' favourite colours, but especially purple. If you want lots of happy bees, plant purple flowers in your flowerpots. Bees are clever because purple flowers are rich in nectar. Bees really enjoy it when large bunches of purple flowers are planted together. They will happily hover and buzz from one flower to the next.

Pesticides and pollinators don't mix

Pesticides are used to stop insects or fungi from eating crops. Natural pesticides have been used for a long time, but stronger chemical pesticides were invented to help farmers grow more crops on bigger farms. Gardening without using chemical pesticides helps pollinators because these pesticides don't just stop the little bugs that eat the crops – they can harm pollinators too.

Soapy water or garlic act like a natural pesticide and can help you in the garden. See page 37 for more on this.

Lights out!

Bees and other insects don't like bright lights in cities and near roads at night. This is called light pollution. It stops some creatures getting a good night's sleep and confuses ones that pollinate after dark, like bats and moths.

People and charities around the world are trying to make friendlier places for pollinators to do their vital work by protecting nature and helping to reduce light pollution.

Animals

Some small animals often carry pollen by mistake. They brush up against a flower and the tiny grains of powder stick to their fur. When they walk past another flower later on, they spread the pollen.

Ants

Ants are cheeky! They like to rob nectar, but they aren't very good at pollinating. They sometimes bring pollen to another flower, but usually they just eat the nectar.

Bats

Bats are important pollinators, especially in hot, tropical places like jungles and deserts. Most of the flowers that bats pollinate open at night. They pollinate over 300 different types of fruits, like mangos, bananas and guavas.

Bees

There are over 16,000 species of bee. Bees are found on every continent in the world except Antarctica. They are the busiest pollinators of all.

Some bees, such as the honeybee, live in hives, while others live alone in little cracks in trees or in the ground. Bumblebees, which have fluffy-looking bodies, are often the easiest bees to spot.

Beetles

The flowers that beetles help to pollinate usually smell really strong because beetles find their way by using their sense of smell. Beetles are attracted to flat, open flowers near the ground, which allow them to easily eat the pollen. Sometimes they pollinate by accident as they scurry about their business.

Ladybirds are a type of beetle, so they can help with pollination too.

Ancient fossils show that beetles and flies were probably the first insect pollinators. They helped to spread the pollen of prehistoric flowers around **150 million** years ago, when dinosaurs roamed the Earth.

Birds

Small birds like hummingbirds feed from flowers by hovering their wings. One tiny bird in Australia that is a good pollinator has a nice name – it's called a honeyeater. When birds like the honeyeater hover their wings, the pollen gets tossed around and falls onto nearby flowers.

Butterflies

Butterflies hop and flitter from flower to flower, gently fluttering their beautiful wings. This helps to spread pollen in the air. It falls on flowers close by.

Flies

While some flies eat crops, which is bad, others can be helpful by moving pollen around on their bodies and wings.

Moths

Pollen can get stuck to a moth's furry body or to its long tongue as it reaches down into a flower looking for nectar. Most moths fly only at night, so you might not notice them as they flit from flower to flower in the dark. Many moths prefer to feed from pale flowers that have a strong smell, which are easier to find on a dark night. Some species of moth can travel long distances, carrying the pollen to other flowers that are far away.

Wasps

Wasps are not as hairy or as fluffy as bees, so they carry less pollen on their bodies. But they still help by flying from one flower to another gathering pollen.

Wind

The wind is also a good pollinator. Gusts of wind help to carry tiny grains of pollen. They float on the breeze from one place to another.

Honeybees

Honeybees are fascinating little creatures. They give us one of our most delicious foods, honey, which they make so they have something to feed on in the winter when there are fewer flowers.

Bees in the hive come close together for the winter, feeding on the honey and waving their wings really fast to keep the hive warm. Luckily, they often make quite a lot of honey, so beekeepers can take some and sell it.

Honey has been found inside the pyramids in Egypt and it was still nice to eat! There are a lot of natural sugars in honey, which help it last a long time without going bad.

The waggle dance

Bees can travel about 3 kilometres (2 miles) from their hive to gather nectar.

When a bee finds a good patch of flowers with lots of nectar, it flies back to its hive to tell the others. They communicate by doing a waggle dance. The other bees understand the dance moves that the bee is making with its body. They know to fly off with it to gather lots of nectar for honey-making.

Eating pollen

Humans can eat pollen that has been dried out. It's difficult to collect, though. Beekeepers attach little pollen traps at each door of a hive. As the bees pass through, the pollen falls from their legs and is collected in a little dish. The beekeeper cleans it, dries it and packages it. You can buy it in jars and sprinkle it on your cereal, porridge or yogurt.

Bee pollen has more protein per gram than red meat!

Rent-a-bee

Farmers in some parts of the world rent beehives and move them onto their land for the pollinating season to help their crops grow. This is usually done by fruit farmers. The beehives arrive overnight. When the bees wake up in the morning, they are in orchards filled with blossoms.

Not all bees live in hives

Because bumblebees don't live in hives, they look for places to hibernate in the autumn and early winter. They often find little holes in the ground or cracks in the bark of a tree to make a cosy sleeping place. They come back out in early spring and start making their summer nests. Provide a safe place for them to hibernate in by making a bumblebee home, like the one on the next page.

Activity: Build a bug house

You will need:
- A large leftover plastic bottle
- A few bamboo canes (you can get these in a garden centre)
- Twigs, bits of bark, moss or pinecones
- Twine (optional)

You can make a nice cosy home for your local pollinators.

1. Ask a grown-up to cut the two ends off the large plastic bottle so that you have a tube about 15cm long. Be careful of the edges in case they are sharp after being cut.
2. Ask an adult to help you cut the hollow bamboo canes so that they are slightly longer than your repurposed plastic tube.
3. Do the same with the twigs.
4. Fill the tube with the hollow bamboo canes and the twigs.
5. Add the bits of bark, moss or pinecones. Pack everything in tightly until the tube is completely full and the sticks have no room to move around.
6. Put the bug house in a quiet spot. You can also tie some twine around it and hang it from a tree.

Pollinators need a water source. They love to see puddles or birdbaths in gardens or near fields. If you have a birdbath, put a small pebble or stone in the centre to give insects a spot to safely perch on while they drink their fill.

Activity: Plant a pollinator party pot

You will need:
- Seeds or small herb plants
- A big flowerpot
- A few handfuls of stones
- Soil

Planting a pollinator-friendly pot of flowers will help the pollinators to party! Try to have at least one plant in flower at any time of year. Winter and early spring are the most challenging times for pollinators, so it's nice to include plants that will flower in those seasons.

Pollinators love herbs, and many herbs grow year-round. The pot can also double up as a mini herb garden for cooking. Thyme, sage, oregano, chives and rosemary are all good choices. Lavender, echinacea, onions, beans and peppers are also great for pollinators.

Borage has blue star-shaped flowers that you can add to a salad or freeze in ice cubes to make a drink look pretty. Bees adore the flowers. Borage can grow tall, so only plant it if you have a big pot or a lot of space.

There are a few planting options: either start with seeds, like you did in the 'Seeds' chapter, go to a shop or garden centre that sells small plants or go to a community garden plant swap. If you plant seeds, you might not be able to harvest all the herbs in the first year as they will still be quite small.

1. Choose a big flowerpot that has a hole in the base. Add a few handfuls of stones in the bottom to help drain water. Herbs don't like soggy soil, so use a soil that drains well, such as a sandy soil.
2. Add soil on top of the stones, leaving room to add your herbs.
3. Press each herb plant down firmly in the soil, then add some more soil around the base of the plants.
4. Water well.
5. Put the pot in a sunny spot.
6. Watch as the bees and other pollinators have a party feeding on all the nectar!

GROWING

Get growing!

Fruit, vegetables and herbs are usually at their best when they have just been picked, so having some growing nearby means you will have fresh food when you want it. Good starter plants to grow are herbs, strawberries, peas, beans, salad leaves, potatoes and courgettes. You can plant these in a flowerpot or in a garden.

Follow the sunshine

If you are choosing a spot to grow your herbs, vegetables or fruit, pick a sheltered place that will get six or more hours of sunlight each day. The sun warms plants as they grow, which helps to create a good crop.

Have you ever noticed that some flowers move their heads to look at the sun? They do this to get as much warmth and energy as they can throughout the day. Having too little sunshine means a plant won't get enough energy. They can become straggly and their fruit and vegetables won't be plump.

Weeds

Weeds are simply plants that are in the wrong place. They are usually plants that grow well in that area. They can crowd out other plants by taking their soil and sunlight, so before you start your growing adventure, remove all the weeds from the area.

HOW DO YOU DO, FELLOW TULIPS?

??

Water your plants

Water is important for almost all living things on our planet. This is especially true for plants that produce food. Most vegetables and fruits have a lot of water inside them, which comes from the rain, from a nearby river or from careful watering. The water is soaked up by the plant's roots, which are deep in the soil.

How much and how often you water your plants will depend on the weather, what type of plants you're growing, the size of the plant and the type of soil. Having water close to your growing area is helpful because you will need to keep the soil moist as your crops grow.

When you're watering plants, pour the water near the roots instead of on top of the leaves to wet the soil evenly. You should also water your plants in the morning or evening instead of in the middle of the day, especially on a hot day – the water can evaporate too quickly and the plant doesn't get a chance to soak up what it needs.

Water butts

If you have room for one, a water butt is a great addition to your garden or balcony. The best place to put one is under a drainpipe that is coming off the roof. The water will collect in the butt on rainy days. Use the water on drier, sunny days to keep your soil nice and damp.

water is important for a lot of our food, not just plants. We catch fish and shellfish in seas and rivers. People also eat seaweed and algae that grow underwater. Rivers do extra work by helping to keep fields wet in the summer.

Dishwater

Use leftover dishwater or water from a bath or paddling pool to water your garden. This will help to save water, which is especially important in hot weather.

When to plant herbs, fruit and vegetables

SUMMER
- CABBAGE · CARROTS · CAULIFLOWER
- CHARD · COURGETTES · CUCUMBER
- KALE · PAK CHOI · PARSNIPS
- PUMPKIN · RADISHES
- SALAD LEAVES
- SPRING ONIONS
- SQUASH

SPRING
- AUBERGINE · BEETROOT · BRUSSELS SPROUTS
- CABBAGE · CARROTS · CAULIFLOWER
- CELERY · CELERIAC · GARLIC · LEEKS
- LETTUCE · SALAD LEAVES
- SPRING ONIONS · POTATOES
- PURPLE SPROUTING BROCCOLI
- SPINACH · SWEETCORN
- TURNIPS

TOMATOES

STRAWBERRIES · TOMATOES

BASIL · CORIANDER · MINT · PARSLEY · ROSEMARY · SAGE · THYME

CHIVES · CORIANDER · PARSLEY

VEGETABLES · FRUIT · HERBS

> Rhubarb grows back every year, but only eat the stems once the plant is over two years old. Don't eat the leaves because they can make you sick.

Fruits like apples, pears, plums, damsons, gooseberries, raspberries, blackcurrants and blackberries either grow on trees or bushes that you can get from garden centres.

Compost

Compost is made up of things like leaves, vegetable peels and other organic matter that has rotted and is added back to the soil to make it richer for growing more vegetables.

Making compost is like following a recipe: you need to put the right stuff in, in the right amounts. The recipe is easy to remember because it needs only two ingredients: green material and brown material. The mix should be half of each.

- Green organic material is made of food scraps, grass trimmings and garden cuttings.
- Brown organic material is made of dried leaves, bits of cardboard and paper or wood chips.

A lot of people don't put any meat, dairy or fish waste in their compost, just scraps from fruit and vegetables.

You should turn your compost with a garden fork every week or so. Turn the compost from the bottom to the top, mixing all the newer things with the older layers and letting air get down through it all. Most garden centres and some recycling centres sell compost bins. Some compost bins have an opening low to the ground and others are easier to turn as you can lift up the lid to put a fork inside.

Eggshells

Eggshells have lots of uses in the garden. Sprinkling broken eggshells near your plants is a good way to annoy hungry snails or slugs. No matter how much they would like to munch your tasty plants, they don't like crawling over the eggshells.

Mixing broken eggshells into your soil will also help to add air, which makes it easier for plants to grow.

As the shells break down in the soil, they provide calcium and other nutrients.

Wash the eggshells in warm water to remove any of the sticky stuff that might be inside them before using them in the garden.

Coffee

The grounds that are left over after making coffee are handy for deterring slugs and snails because they don't like how the texture feels on their bellies. Sprinkle used coffee grounds on the soil once the coffee has cooled down. The coffee grounds also add richness to the soil and make it more acidic.

Soapy solution

Early in the growing season, plants are healthy and blossoming. As the weather gets hotter, more and more bugs and some diseases start to damage the plants, but soapy water can stop them. Adding a squirt of dishwashing liquid to a spray bottle, topping it up with water and spraying your plants with it will help to keep off most bugs. You can also add a few garlic cloves to the bottle for extra protection.

Ladybirds are also great at keeping little bugs away, so if you see ladybirds in your garden, say hello and ask them to stay.

Rest on a stone

Putting large, flat stones under pumpkins or big courgettes as they grow will stop them from going bad. The stone will capture heat from the sun and keep the bottom of the vegetable warm and dry.

Potatoes

You can grow new potato plants from some spuds in your cupboard. You do this by chitting them, which means allowing little green sprouts to form on your potatoes.

1. To chit your potatoes, put them in an open egg carton and leave them to sit in a cool, bright place for about three weeks, until the sprouts are about 1.5cm long.
2. Plant the potatoes in nice rich soil. They can be planted in an old compost bag or a big sack.
3. You will need to cover the leaves with soil when they first appear (this is called earthing up), then harvest the potatoes a few weeks later.
4. Early potatoes (planted in March) can be harvested in July. Hot and humid weather later in the summer can cause the potatoes to get sick from a disease called potato blight.

SPROUTS

Climate

Different foods grow in different climates. Pineapples grow in a tropical climate, but a pear or an apple needs a cooler place to grow.

Climate describes the weather over a long period of time. The climate in a jungle is usually tropical, which means the weather is hot and wet, whereas the climate in the North and South Poles will be freezing for most of the year. The climate in a region usually stays the same from one century to the next, but climate change means that the type of weather in some parts of the world is changing.

Gravitational pull

Plants can sense the Earth's gravitational pull. This helps them to know which way to send their roots and shoots in the dark soil. The roots push further down into earth. The shoots push upwards and break through the ground to reach towards the sunshine.

People began to farm about **11,000** years ago.

Farming

Farming allowed humans to settle in one place. Before crops were farmed, people moved around to catch food. They were called hunter-gatherers. Staying in one place to plant and harvest crops, and to farm animals, made it easier to care for children and have a family.

The future of farming

Today, farmers can use robots on their farms to help them keep an eye on how things are growing or what their animals are doing. There are robots that will milk the cows and tell the farmer if a cow is feeling unwell. Other robots can pick fruit or test the soil.

Protecting plants from the elements

When it's cold and windy outside, vegetable plants prefer to grow inside a glasshouse or polytunnel. The glasshouse or tunnel protects the plants when they are small and provides heat and warmth as they grow. A lot of people who grow vegetables or fruit to sell in shops use a glasshouse or polytunnel so they can grow and sell food all year round.

Glasshouses

Glasshouses have been used for hundreds of years. If you visit a botanical garden, you might be able to see some big, beautiful glasshouses that were built a couple of hundred years ago. The first ones were quite fancy, with their own wood burners or underground heating pipes.

Long before shipping containers could deliver food safely around the world, glasshouses grew fruit, like oranges, for wealthy people. They were also used to grow plants to make medicine.

Polytunnels

Polytunnels are used instead of glasshouses on modern farms. They are made of plastic instead of glass. They are semi-circular and are big enough to walk inside. Plastic is stretched over metal beams, which makes the tunnels waterproof.
If you ever see a polytunnel, you might notice that most of them face north to south. This is so that they get an even amount of sunshine on each side throughout the day.

Creeping underground

Plants grow in thousands of different ways and their roots are different too.

Asparagus grows in an interesting way. It's called a rhizome because its roots move just beneath the soil and the tips of the asparagus poke up from this long root. Other edible rhizomes are ginger and turmeric.

Perennial plants

Asparagus is called a perennial plant because it grows back every year. Perennial plants take a break over the cold months of winter. They keep their roots as warm as they can under the soil, but the leaves and branches fall off until the following spring, when the plant starts to grow towards the sunshine again.

Annual plants

Perennial plants usually have much longer roots than annual plants, which grow for just one year. A carrot is an example of an annual plant. Once it's picked, the plant doesn't grow back again. To get more carrots the next year, you need to save seeds from the flowers on top of the carrot plant and plant them.

Activity: Make a mini polytunnel

You will need:
- Large, empty plastic bottles
- Strong scissors

When you first bring seedlings outside, they can quickly get eaten by slugs and snails because they are so small. To help prevent this, ask an adult to cut the bottom off a large empty plastic bottle to make a mini polytunnel to protect your seedling. Push the cut side down into the soil so the top of the bottle covers your seedling.

This will also protect your seedling from wind and keep it warm. Once your seedling looks bigger and stronger, take the mini polytunnel away.

Activity: DIY watering can

You will need:
- An empty 2-litre milk container
- Chopping board
- Hammer
- Small nail

Make a homemade watering can out of a recycled milk container.

1. Reuse a 2-litre milk container with a handle on the side.
2. Clean the container and take off the label.
3. Ask an adult to make holes in the lid by using a chopping board and hammering a small nail into the lid to make about eight holes.
4. Ask the adult to make one small hole in the handle of the plastic container. This will let some air in and allow water to move about inside the bottle.
5. Fill your new watering can with water and tip it on its side to water your plants.

Activity: Map a vegetable patch

You will need:

- A large sheet of paper or your activity notebook

Map out a place where vegetables could grow. Think about how this would change next year if you're planning to rotate the crops.

Crops are rotated to stop the soil in a plot or field running out of nutrients. One plant can absorb lots of nutrients, but another plant does not. For example, a crop rotation could look like this:

- Year 1: Tomatoes
- Year 2: Onions
- Year 3: Beans
- Year 4: Cabbage

Crop rotation also stops pests and diseases from getting stronger each year. Most diseases like a certain plant and will attack it each year, but if the plants are changed around, the disease won't be able to spread.

How to draw your veg patch

1. Get a large sheet of paper or use your activity notebook.
2. Think of the vegetables you want to plant, then look at the family chart on the next page to group the vegetables into their families.
3. Divide your drawing into four equal-sized plots. Put each vegetable family in a different plot.
4. Find out what type of soil each of these families likes. Some families, like the potato family, are 'hungry' plants that need lots of natural fertilizers and plant food. Other families, like carrots, are not as 'hungry'.

Potato family:
Aubergine, pepper/chilli, potato, tomato

Cucumber family:
Courgette, cucumber, marrow, melon, pumpkin, winter squash

Carrot family:
Carrot, parsley, parsnip

Beet family:
Beetroot, chard, spinach

Lettuce family:
Artichoke, lettuce

Onion family:
Garlic, leek, onion, spring onion

Cabbage family:
Brussels sprouts, cabbage, cauliflower, kale, pak choi, purple sprouting broccoli, radish, rocket, swede, turnip

Pea/bean family:
Asparagus, broad bean, French bean, mangetout, pea, runner bean, sugar snap pea

PICKING

When is the best time to pick food?

SUMMER

Vegetables: Aubergine · Baby Beetroot · Beans · Cabbage · Celery · Chard · Courgettes · Cucumber · Kale · Lettuce · New Potatoes · Pak Choi · Peas · Radishes · Salad Leaves · Spinach · Spring Onions

Fruit: Gooseberries · Raspberries · Strawberries · Tomatoes

Herbs: Basil · Chives · Coriander · Mint · Parsley · Rosemary · Sage · Thyme

SPRING

Vegetables: Asparagus · Beans · Cabbage · Kale · Onions · Purple Sprouting Broccoli

Fruit: Rhubarb

Herbs: Mint · Rosemary · Sage · Thyme

VEGETABLES   FRUIT   HERBS

※ Look at the rainbow to see when you should pick the food you've grown. Some people plant their seeds a little earlier than others, so their vegetables could be ready a bit earlier. The amount of sun, the temperature or the type of soil that plants grow in will also have an effect. Each year, the weather is a little different – the sun is out longer, it's hotter or colder than usual or it rains more from one year to the next. This diagram gives you an idea of when things will be ready, but your vegetables might act a little differently.

AUTUMN

Beans · Beetroot · Cabbage · Cauliflower · Celery · Carrots · Courgettes · Cucumber · Chard · Kale · Leeks · Lettuce · Garlic · Pak Choi · Potatoes · Onions · Purple Sprouting Broccoli · Radishes · Salad Leaves · Spinach · Spring Onions · Squash · Sweetcorn · Turnips

Apples · Blackberries · Blackcurrants · Damsons · Gooseberries · Pears · Plums · Strawberries · Tomatoes

Chives · Mint · Parsley · Rosemary · Sage · Thyme

WINTER

Brussels Sprouts · Cabbage · Carrots · Cauliflower · Celeriac · Garlic · Kale · Leeks · Pak Choi · Parsnips · Pumpkin · Salad Leaves · Spring Onions · Squash · Turnips

Rosemary · Sage · Thyme

HERBS   FRUIT

There are a few tricks that you can learn to tell when your vegetables are ready for picking.

Early riser

It's usually best to harvest fruit and vegetables early in the morning. This is when they are sweetest and juiciest because they plump up with moisture overnight.

Be careful

If vegetables or fruit don't come off their stalks easily when you gently twist or pull them, use a scissors or hand pruners. This will also stop the plant from breaking or tearing.

Avoid wet weather

Don't pick on a wet day. If there is a disease or a fungus on a plant, picking it when there is rain on the leaves can spread the disease and make other plants sick. Berries picked in the rain will have extra water inside them that has come through their thin skin. This will make them go off sooner than ones picked on a dry day.

Keep on picking

Strangely enough, with many plants, the more you pick, the more fruit the plant will make. A plant's goal is to reproduce, and the fruit and vegetables are created to help them do this. If the plant is already full of fruit, there is no reason for it to make more. But if you pick the fruit, it will start to make more, and you will have more fresh food for longer.

Bigger isn't always better

Some plants need to be picked straight away when they ripen, but others can wait on the stalk or in the ground for a little longer. Many foods, such as beans, peas and turnips, are tastiest and full of goodness when they are small and tender. Others, such as tomatoes, courgettes and pumpkins, taste good when they are allowed to ripen on the plants so that their flavours can fully develop. But once they get their bright colour, they are ready. Courgettes are great for picking when they are about 20cm long.

You can eat the beautiful yellow flowers from a courgette plant. They can be stuffed with cheese, deep-fried or added to a salad.

Outer green leaves

Unless you are pulling the whole plant out of the ground, you should harvest the outer, larger leaves of leafy vegetables such as pak choi, chard, kale or lettuce before picking the ones closer to the centre. These leafy vegetables sprout and grow from the centre of the plant, so picking the outer leaves first will allow the plant to keep growing in the centre and continue to sprout more and more leaves for you.

Carrots

The top of the carrot will usually start to pop up through the soil when it's getting ready to be picked. You will see the tops turning a nice bright orange (or yellow if you planted yellow carrots). A small garden fork is an ideal tool for harvesting carrots or other root crops such as potatoes or parsnips.

The leafy tops of the carrots can be eaten too! See the recipe for carrot top pesto on page 83.

Peas in a pod

There are lots of different types of peas, so some will look different to others when they are fully ripe. But you will usually see the little peas swelling up inside their pods. With the popular variety called mangetout, the seeds will be small. Other varieties, like sugar snap, will swell up with a line of big peas inside.

Tip-top tomatoes

When your tomatoes are ripe, they should be shiny and glossy and they should smell lovely and tomatoey. When you press them, they should be firm, not squishy, but not **too** hard. When you pick them, they should come off the plant easily.

Travelling all around the world

A gardener can harvest or pick their fruit or vegetables when they are ripe and at their best, but farmers often have to pick food before it's ripe so that it can be transported around the world. Some fruit and vegetables ripen as they travel in shipping containers or on the back of a lorry instead of in the sunshine. This can change the taste and amount of goodness in the food.

A glut

A glut means that you have lots of one thing ripening at the same time. In fact, you'll have so much that you can't possibly eat it all. There are a lot of things you can do when this happens. Some people pop foods in their freezer until they need them a few weeks later. You can make jam and other things like relish or chutney that last a long time. Or you can make some lovely fruit tarts. If you have a glut of tomatoes, try making your own tomato sauce using the recipe on page 86.

Keeping fresh

Fruit and vegetables all like to be stored in different ways. Lots of foods are best kept in the fridge, where they can stay nice and cold, such as strawberries, raspberries, peas, beans and especially lettuce. The less you handle these fruits and vegetables after harvesting, the longer they will last.

Other things, like onions and garlic, like to stay outside of the fridge. They need a cool, dark place to dry out after they have been picked. Once dried, they can be stored for a few months.

Tough herbs like thyme or rosemary keep well after being picked if you stand them in a glass of water. You can also dry these herbs on a plate. For softer herbs like coriander and basil, store them in the fridge after you pick them. Wrap them in some damp kitchen paper and put them in an airtight container before putting them in the fridge.

Activity: Find a rainbow

You will need:
- A six-hole egg carton
- 6 different, bright paint colours
- A paintbrush

This activity is a chance to look at the different ways that plants grow and the wonderful variety of food they provide us with.

1. Paint each hole in the egg carton with a different colour of the rainbow and allow it to dry.
2. Take your painted egg carton to the garden or to a park or community garden with an adult. Walk around looking for items that are the same colours as the colours in your carton. You might find baby spinach leaves, a gooseberry or a fluffy piece of a fennel plant, which are all bright green. Or you might find raspberries or lettuce leaves that are deep red.

Activity: Pick a pizza

You will need:
- Pebbles or stones
- Oregano plants
- Tomato plants
- Spring onion plants
- Rocket plants
- Basil plants

1. Make a large circular outline in the soil with pebbles or stones. Mark out 'pizza slices' by making lines of stones from the outside to the centre of the circle.
2. Plant oregano in one of the slices, tomatoes in another, spring onions in the next one and rocket in the next. Basil is also good on top of a pizza.
3. Try to plant a variety of tomato that won't grow too tall.
4. When you pick your herbs and tomatoes, you will have your own home-grown pizza toppings!

TASTING

The five tastes

Humans can detect five different tastes: sweet, salty, sour, bitter and umami. Being able to taste food helps us to stay healthy because it helps us to enjoy what we're eating. Our senses also help us know when something has gone bad.

Sweet

Almost everyone loves sweet food. Your body is designed to be happy when you taste sugary foods like honey or ripe fruit – a signal is sent to your brain and to your gut when you eat them. Scientists think we like sweet foods so much because they can provide our bodies with lots of energy by making glucose. Babies are born liking sweet-tasting things and breastmilk is sweet.

Children should have less than 5 teaspoons of sugar a day, but it's hard to know how much sugar we actually eat because a lot of it can be hidden inside our food. For example, tomato ketchup has a lot of sugar in it. So do most of the cereals that come in boxes. Sweet drinks can also be full of sugar.

Salty

Salt is important to help your body function. It helps your muscles and nerves to work properly. It also helps to balance the amount of water in your body.

We get salt from our food, but like sugar, you shouldn't eat too much salt – you need less than a teaspoon a day. It's difficult to guess how much salt you eat every day because there is a lot of salt added to the processed foods that we buy.

Sour and bitter

Sour and bitter can be confusing. A sour taste is caused by acidic flavours like lemons, yogurt or vinegar. Bitter is a sharp taste like dark chocolate, cabbage, coffee and black tea.

SOUR

BITTER

Umami

Umami is a Japanese word that is used to describe the taste you experience when you eat something like bacon, cheese or soy sauce. It's a savoury taste that makes food taste delicious.

Umami was only made an official taste in the 1990s, when scientists found the taste-buds that can detect it. Scientists are still studying how taste works on our tongue. We might even learn about more new tastes in the future.

Taste-buds

Taste-buds are sensitive little bumps on your tongue that send messages to your brain about how something tastes. They let you know if the food is sweet, sour, bitter, salty or umami.

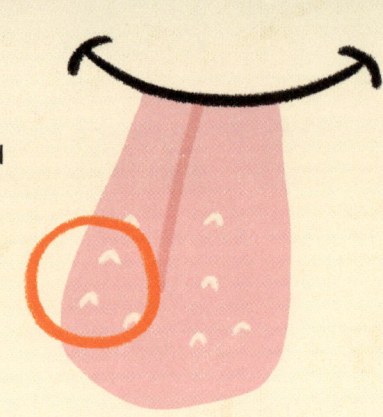

Most adults have about 10,000 taste-buds. Your body replaces your taste-buds every two weeks or so. When you get older, some of those taste cells don't get replaced. Because of this, a lot of older people have only 5,000 taste-buds. Babies and children, however, have a lot more – they have about 30,000 taste-buds. That's why some foods taste much stronger to children than they do to adults.

Don't forget your nose!

Your nose and sense of smell also play an important part in how you taste your food. While you are chewing, food releases chemicals that travel up into your nose. These chemicals cause a reaction inside your nose that helps to create the true flavour of your food. Have you ever noticed that if you have a bad cold or a stuffy nose, it's hard to taste your food? Experiment by holding your nose when you eat something – does blocking the smell make a difference to the taste?

> Some adults have more than **10,000** taste-buds. These people are called supertasters. Foods taste very strong to them, especially bitter foods.

How tastes become flavours

A flavour is different to a taste. Taste is just the little receptors in your mouth reacting to the food. Flavour is more complicated because it's taste mixed with the smell of the food and how the food affects your body.

For example, when you eat a sweet food like a peach, the flavour of it comes from the taste of it in your mouth as well as the smell of its sweetness when you bite into its soft skin. Your brain brings this information together from your senses to tell you the flavour of the peach.

Flavourists

A flavourist studies different flavours. They use science to make new food flavours or they try to copy ones that we already know, like making strawberry or orange flavouring to be added to foods.

We all taste differently

We all have different genes and they affect how we taste things. For example, some people find the taste of coriander very strong and think it tastes like soap, while others think it tastes delicious and they love sprinkling it all over a curry. Some people can eat lots of sour foods, while others find it difficult.

How often you eat a food is important too. If you grow up in a country with more bitter or sour-tasting food, you'll get used to those tastes. If you try a food again and again, you will probably end up liking it.

Scientists say we need to taste something **12 times** to go from not liking a food to liking it.

Hot and spicy

Spicy isn't a flavour or a taste – it's actually a signal that your nerves send to your brain to tell you that something is making your mouth hot and uncomfortable. The signal is sent from little receptors inside your mouth. Some people have a lot fewer of these receptors than others, so they can eat much spicier food.

Mouthfeel

We taste food with our senses, but another thing that makes us like food is how it feels in our mouth. This is called mouthfeel. Chocolate is silky and smooth when it melts on our tongue, which is one of the reasons it's so popular.

Other things have a nice crunchy texture, like crisps, or a soft, pleasing mouthfeel, like cake.

Using all your senses to explore food

We use all five senses when exploring the food that we eat. We can see, feel, smell, hear and taste our food. For example, when you pick up a shiny pepper, you see the bright red colour and feel the smooth texture. You can smell the sweetness of a strawberry and hear the snap of a carrot breaking before listening to the crunch of it in your mouth.

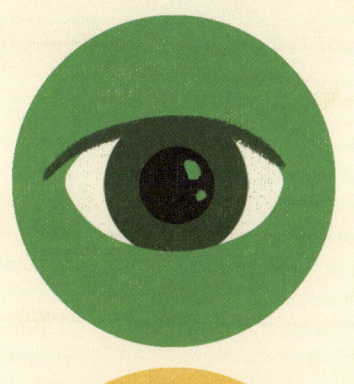

Taste the colour

When a food is a different colour than you expect, your brain tells you that it tastes different too. The taste and flavour of the food are affected by what you see.

For example, adding a pinkish-red colour will make a drink or food seem sweeter, while green can make us think a food is sour. You might think it tastes like limes even if it isn't lime flavoured.

Another funny thing that happens is that we eat a lot more if we see different colours together. Scientists have discovered that if you have a packet of sweets with lots of colours inside, you keep eating. But if there is just one colour, you slow down after a while and eat fewer sweets.

Food memories

When you think of foods that someone you love made for you or when you remember a special meal, it makes you happy because your brain releases a chemical called dopamine. These food memories help you to enjoy certain foods more than others and can make you feel good. These are called comfort foods.

Activity: Taste test

You will need:
- 5 small glasses
- Salt
- Sugar
- Soy sauce
- Lemon juice
- Tonic water
- A piece of paper or your activity notebook

1. Fill two small glasses with warm water. Stir 1 teaspoon of salt into one glass and 1 teaspoon of sugar into the other glass.

2. Put cold water into two more glasses. Add 1 teaspoon of soy sauce to one glass and 1 teaspoon of lemon juice to the other glass.

3. Pour some tonic water into the fifth glass.

4. Take a tiny taste from each glass, one at a time. Can you identify what taste it is? Remember, the tastes are salty, sweet, umami, sour and bitter. Write a list of words to describe the different tastes on a piece of paper or in your activity notebook.

5. Try tasting from all the glasses a second time, but this time, hold your nose as you do. Write down any differences in this experience. What did you learn?

Activity: Taste a rainbow

You will need:
- A selection of colourful fruit and vegetables
- A piece of paper or your activity notebook

1. Ask an adult to help you gather a selection of colourful fruit and vegetables. Try to get as many colours of the rainbow as possible. Put them on a table.

2. Look at the colours and chat about the brightness and different types of colours. Write down a description of each food in your activity notebook or on a piece of paper. For example, pick up a shiny pepper and feel the texture, then write a description.

3. Smell each piece of food and describe it. For example, you could describe the sweetness of a strawberry.

4. Hearing your food may seem more unusual, but you can hear a pea pod pop open if you squeeze it.

5. If you would like to, you can taste all the foods that you have laid out, but tasting is not essential. If you don't like the taste of something straight away, it's worth trying it a few times – you might like it eventually! (Remember what scientists said about trying a food 12 times before you like it?)

6. While you are doing this activity, write down all the words that could describe each food. For example, is it shiny, smelly, noisy, crinkly, soft or squishy?

BUYING

How does food get to your kitchen?

The food system is the name for all the things that link together to impact what we eat. There are so many different things that it's hard to name them all, but we can try!

What we eat affects the planet

How food is grown can help the environment or it can harm it. Things that harm the environment are chemical fertilizers and too much of one plant in an area, which reduces biodiversity.

More and more farmers are trying to make sure that what they do is good for the land and the environment. Some farmers use organic methods, which means they use very few chemicals. You can buy organic food in most shops.

Throughout history, certain foods have been used as edible money. Ancient Mayan people from Central America used cocoa beans as money – these are the beans we use to make chocolate today.

Cow burps

A cow's stomach is split into four parts, which means they burp a lot! These burps are methane gas, which is one type of the greenhouse gas emissions that cause global warming. The more beef or hamburgers or steak we eat, the more cows are raised and the more methane is produced from all their burps.

Shop local

Some of the foods that we enjoy eating, such as bananas and mangos, grow in hot climates. A long time ago, most people only ate food that could be grown locally. Nowadays, because of global transport, it's normal to eat food that has travelled thousands of miles.

If you look at the fresh food in your local shop, you will see that some of it has travelled across the world to get there. Lots of things grow in one part of the world but not another, so it makes sense for those foods to travel. Bananas and pineapples, for example, will never grow in a cold climate. But other foods can be grown closer to where they are sold. Farmers can then bring food to a market and sell directly to people.

—you

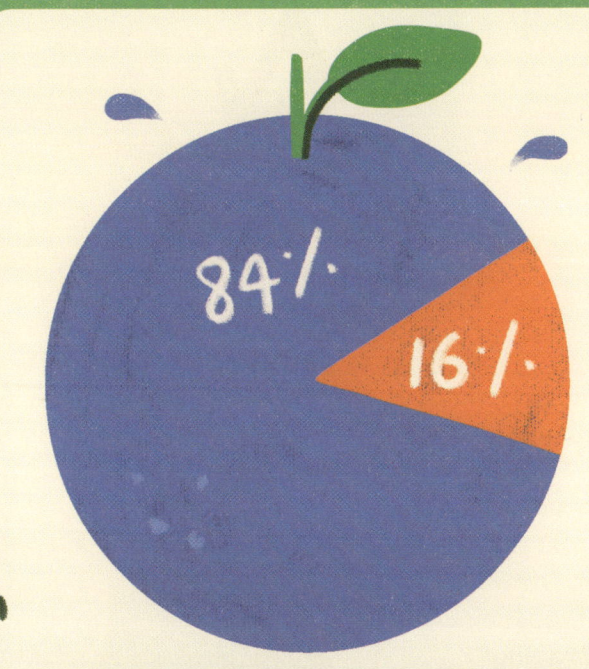

Eating water

We eat water as well as drinking it. Water is transported around the world within fruit and vegetables.

For example, an apple is **84% water**, an orange is **87% water** and a cucumber is **96% water**. When a cucumber is grown and watered in Italy and then transported to another country, a lot of the water that was used to water the plant travels inside it and then we eat that water.

Food packaging

Packaging helps food last longer. It keeps it fresh by keeping air away from it. Packaging helps us move food from one place to another without damaging it. It also allows us to stack food neatly on shop shelves.

Paper and cardboard are the most popular ways to package food. In the 1970s, plastic started to become popular and is now used for packaging a huge number of things like yogurts and chocolate bars. Plastic netting is used for fruit. Glass jars and bottles and metal containers are also used. So are wooden boxes that can be stacked full of heavy items like oranges or bottles of apple juice.

Recycling

If you look around your kitchen, you will notice that much of the packaging can be recycled. This packaging usually has a symbol on it to tell you that you can put it in a recycling bin.

Packaging for the compost

Some food companies are becoming more aware of the environment and are starting to experiment with packaging that can go in the compost bin. They are using things like milk, seaweed, vegetable fats, corn, sawdust, woodchips and even leftover coffee grinds to make food packaging.

Shipping containers

The invention of shipping containers made it much easier to transport food (and everything else too) around the world. Shipping containers were invented by Malcom McLean. He owned a company with lots of trucks and was annoyed at how long it took to take food off each truck and then load it onto a ship. He invented a container that could be filled up at a factory or on a farm, put onto the back of a truck and then lifted from the truck onto a ship with a big crane. This saved a lot of time. It also made it cheaper to ship foods like bananas and avocados from warm countries to other parts of the world, which then made them cheaper to buy.

Ultra-processed or industrial foods

Packaging, shipping and science have helped to create industrial foods that are much different from something you could make in your kitchen at home. These ultra-processed or industrial foods are designed to last a long time and to be easy to transport. This type of food is not as nutritious as food that is grown on a farm or in a garden. It's often made by adding fat, sugar and salt to make it taste good.

Clever advertising

Food companies sell food in clever ways so that we will buy their food instead of food from another company. They do this by advertising on the internet, on TV or with posters near schools or on buses.

Food companies spend billions on advertising, a number so big that it's hard to imagine – it's one thousand million! They wouldn't spend this money if advertising didn't work, so it's worth thinking about the reasons why they do this.

People working in advertising know that children can help their parents make decisions about what they want to eat, so they advertise children's food.

When you watch a movie and see packaged food and drinks being eaten by the movie stars, this was organised by food companies so that the food looks good and people will want to buy it because famous people are eating it.

The magic of colour

Companies make food attractive by using colour on the packaging. This is called colour psychology.

- People often eat more food and eat it more quickly when they are surrounded by red because the colour red increases your heart rate.
- Green packaging makes people think the food is healthy.
- Orange and yellow on the packaging can make people feel hungry.

Temptation

Putting things like sweets and crisps on shelves so that they are easy to see is a way of tempting people to buy them. Shops make a lot of money when they sell sweets and they know that we all like to eat them. When you are waiting to pay for your shopping, there are rows of sweets at the checkout to tempt you.

Supermarkets also play tricks by pumping out sweet baking smells at the front of the shop. The smell can make your tummy rumble and it tempts you to buy cakes and bread.

There is no such thing as 'kids' food'!

Humans of all ages need food that helps them to grow and be as happy and healthy as they can be. When you're young, you are growing fast and need lots of good food to help with this. Sometimes food is called 'kids' food' and it often comes in a bright package. But there is really no such thing as special food for kids. Everyone just needs nutritious, tasty food.

Activity: How meals connect us

You will need:
- A piece of paper or your activity notebook
- A map of the world

1. Think about your favourite meal. Draw a picture of it on a piece of paper or in your activity notebook.
2. Make a list of all the main ingredients.
3. Use a map of the world and some detective skills to find out where these ingredients grew or where they were made, then look at how they travelled around the planet.
4. Find out about different cultures that use each ingredient in their food and what meals they make with it (an adult can help you to look up this information). Are they similar to the food in the meal you have drawn in your notebook?

You can travel the world from your kitchen! Do this by planning to eat food from a different country one day each week or one day a month. Start by exploring different recipes and ingredients from the country you have chosen. You might discover Lebanese falafel, a tasty French specialty, have fun making a sushi roll or create a delicious pad thai from Thailand. You can also look at how people from each country eat together or how they set the table before a meal.

Activity: Food miles detective

> **You will need:**
> - A piece of paper or your activity notebook
> - Fruit and vegetable packaging labels
> - A map of the world
> - A calculator

Food miles are the distance that food has travelled to get to your kitchen or onto your plate.

Use the same meal you drew for the last activity or pick a different meal if you prefer. This time you're going to be an air miles detective and see how far all the food has travelled to get to your plate.

1. If some of the ingredients have come in a packet, the packet will say what country it was made in. Write the country down beside the ingredients in your list. Fruit and vegetables might have a label or a sticker telling you where the food was grown.

2. Work out how far it is from your home country or hometown to where the food came from, then write down the distance each item has travelled. Add up all these numbers to find the number of air miles in your meal.

3. You can also think about the way the food was grown. Could it be grown closer to your home? An adult might help you find a carbon emissions calculator online, which will help you work out the distances as well as the carbon footprint of the food.

COOKING

Building blocks of cooking

Like anything else that you have learned, like riding a bike or reading a book, learning to cook takes a bit of practice and a lot of help. Once you learn a few skills and start to know what certain ingredients taste like, you can make up your own recipes or start to change recipes to include your favourite foods.

Once you know how to make a simple meal, it can save you money and you will be able to cook for your family and friends. Cooking a meal for someone and sharing food together is a nice way of showing you care.

Cave people were the first cooks

Cooking was invented by cave people more than 1 million years ago. Cooking food over fire helped them digest it more easily. Over a very long time, humans' jaw muscles and guts began to get smaller because the cooked foods were easier to eat. This allowed human brains to start getting bigger, which in turn allowed us to develop into the humans we are today.

Dine In

TABLE: _____ #: _____

Chefs often use creative ways to make food. They can work in huge teams and spend hours getting a meal just right. In some of the fanciest restaurants in the world, there are more chefs in the kitchen than customers in the dining room!

What will we cook in the future?

In the future, we will all probably eat more insects. Lots of people around the world eat them now, but they will become more popular because they are full of protein, which helps strengthen your muscles and bones and gives you energy. Insects are also environmentally sustainable because they grow fast and are cold-blooded, so they don't need warm places to grow. Also, they don't need as much water, land or food as chickens, cows or other animals. We will probably start to make foods like cereals and flapjacks from insect flour. Insects will also be useful when trying to feed people living in harsh environments, such as on the edge of a desert or in a refugee camp.

Food and recipes cross the globe and help to connect people. They can also bring back memories of home if someone moves to another country.

Let's get started!

- If you're using anything sharp or hot, ask an adult to help you. In fact, if you are unsure of anything, ask for help. Things like chopping food, opening tins, heating up pans, taking things out of the oven and draining boiling water can be tricky when you're learning how to cook.

- Hot ovens, pots and pans and sharp knives should always be treated with care, even as you get older and more confident.

- Before you start cooking, always wash your hands well.

- Get all your equipment and ingredients ready before you start to cook a recipe.

- Always wash your fresh fruits and vegetables before you cook or bake with them.

- Put a damp tea towel under your chopping board so that it doesn't move around as you're cutting food on it.

- When chopping food, curl your fingers in a claw shape to protect them from accidental cuts – see the diagram on page 76.

- Season your food with salt and pepper as you're cooking rather than just at the end.

- When you're baking, you need to use the exact amounts of ingredients called for in the recipe. When you cook something, it's usually okay to add extra ingredients. If you add some extra carrots to a stir-fry or some extra herbs to a rainbow wrap, it won't matter too much. But if you add extra flour when you're making bread or a cake, it won't turn out nicely.

Skills

Building your ability in the kitchen will boost your confidence. Once you have learned a few skills, you will be on your way to becoming a good cook. Learning to use kitchen equipment safely is important, but the most important thing is to always ask an adult before you start cooking and to ask for help when you need it.

Grating

Start to practise grating with a soft vegetable like a courgette or with a block of cheese. When you are grating, you need to press the food up against the grater. The harder the food, the more pressure you need to apply, so starting with a soft food will help you learn this skill.

Put a damp tea towel under a chopping board before you start. This is important because it will stop the chopping board from slipping as you grate your food. Put your grater on the chopping board to catch the food as you grate it.

Hold the top of the grater with one hand (the hand you don't write with). With your other hand, press your food firmly at the top of the grater, then slowly drag it downwards.

Always stop grating before the piece of food in your hand gets too small, otherwise your fingers might touch the grater and get cut.

A box grater has four different sides and each side grates differently. Experiment with each side to see the differences.

Peeling

Hold the peeler in your strong hand (the hand you write with). If you're peeling something long, like a carrot or parsnip, hold the top half of the vegetable and peel the bottom half by moving the peeler downwards, away from your hand. Then turn the vegetable around and do the top half.

If you're peeling something round, like an apple or a potato, put your thumb on one side and one finger on the other and turn the piece of food around as you peel it.

Crushing garlic

You can crush garlic using a garlic crusher. First, take the thin layer of skin off the garlic clove. If you have a really big clove, cut it in half and crush each half separately because you need to use a lot of force to crush a big one.

Chopping

Put a damp tea towel under a chopping board before you start. This will stop the board from slipping as you chop.

One method of chopping uses a claw grip to keep your fingers tucked in, away from the knife. Use the hand you don't write with to hold the food. Tuck your fingers into a claw shape. Hold the knife in your other hand, then steadily chop. The tucked-in fingers will help to hold the edge of the knife in place. As you chop, turn and put the vegetable on its flattest side.

WAYS TO CHOP

- LARGE DICE
- ROUGHLY CHOPPED
- THICKLY SLICED
- SMALL DICE
- FINELY CHOPPED
- THINLY SLICED
- MINCED

Sautéing

Sautéing means gently frying something in hot oil in a pan to bring out the flavour of what you're cooking. You can sauté all sorts of food, like vegetables, meat and fish. Different vegetables take different times to cook, but all sautéing takes patience, as you want the flavours of the food to cook slowly and gently.

A mixture of sautéed onions, celery and carrots is used at the beginning of a lot of dishes from all over the world. Knowing how to make this is a first step in learning how to cook many different things. In France people call it mirepoix, but other countries use names like soffritto or battuto. There are some differences – people can use garlic or peppers, for example, or ginger and chilli are used in Asia – but they are basically the same.

To make a sautéed mirepoix, you will need one medium-sized onion, one medium-sized carrot and one medium-sized stick of celery. Peel the onion and carrot and trim the bottom and top off the celery. Carefully chop all the veg into small dice, keeping them separate.

Add a tablespoon of olive oil or butter to a pan and put it on the hob over a low heat. Once the oil is hot or the butter has melted, add the onion and stir it for about 30 seconds, then add the carrot and celery. Slowly cook the vegetables until they are beginning to soften. Turn down the heat if the vegetables start to stick or burn. When sautéing, you don't want the colour to change too much, except for the onion – you want that to become see-through.

You can pop a lid on the pan as your food sautés to keep it moist. This is called sweating your ingredients.

Seasoning

Seasoning is used in savoury cooking and some baking too. We season food to bring out the flavours and to help them blend together. If you add too much salt the food won't taste good, but if there is too little salt it will taste like something is missing from your dish.

The best trick is to add a little seasoning while cooking, then test your food at the very end to make sure it tastes correct. If you're making different parts of a dish, season each part as you go. Only add a little salt and pepper rather than a lot. You can always add more seasoning, but you can't take it out!

Sometimes recipes say to add salt and pepper 'to taste'. This means that you take a little spoonful of the food you're cooking and let it cool a little. You then taste it to see if it needs any more salt or pepper. You are using your sense of taste to make the decision.

— YOU HAVE GREAT TASTE

— THANKS —

Herbs and spices

Herbs and spices add flavour to your cooking and make your food taste extra-special. Getting to know the different tastes can really help you in the kitchen. You can use either fresh or dried herbs.

Herbs are the leafy parts of certain plants that have strong flavours, such as basil, thyme, coriander and rosemary. When herbs are dried, their flavour gets much stronger, so you need just one or two pinches of dried herbs.

Spices are the seeds, bark, fruit or roots of some plants. Spices include seeds like caraway, cumin, fennel, poppy, sesame and vanilla. Cinnamon is the bark of a tree and ginger is a root. Spices help to build up an appetite for your food, as they not only add flavour but also wonderful smells.

Roasting

Roasting means cooking something in the oven. It works well for things that take a long time to cook, such as a chicken or a big piece of meat. It's also a good way to cook hard vegetables like carrots, parsnips and potatoes. It can take a bit of time to roast food, but the oven does most of the work. You prepare the food at the beginning, put it in the oven, check on it once or twice and then take it out when it's done.

You need to preheat your oven before putting your food in it, then time how long it takes to cook. Different foods take different amounts of time. Most recipes will tell you how much time is needed and will also tell you the temperature the oven should be set at.

Put your food on the middle shelf of the oven so that the heat can flow all around it as it roasts. Not all dishes can be used in a hot oven, so ask an adult for one that is oven-safe.

How to cook rice

Rice is served with a lot of different dinners, like curries and stir-fries, or it can be used to make fried rice. It's the most popular food in the world and people from different countries cook it in different ways.

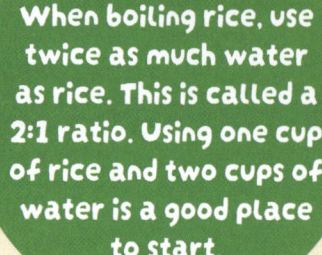

When boiling rice, use twice as much water as rice. This is called a 2:1 ratio. Using one cup of rice and two cups of water is a good place to start.

1. Put the rice and water in a saucepan and put it on the hob over a medium heat. Bring to a boil.
2. Once the water is boiling, give it a stir, then put a lid on your saucepan. Turn the heat down to low and allow the rice to simmer (to boil gently) for about 10 minutes for white rice or 30 minutes for brown rice. You will see small holes appearing on the top of the rice in the saucepan when it's cooked and all the water will have soaked into the rice.
3. Turn off the heat. Leave the rice in the saucepan with the lid on for another 2 minutes to finish steaming.
4. Don't stir rice while it simmers because it can make it turn sticky. Some recipes add a knob of butter or a spoonful of oil at the start of cooking to help separate the grains from each other. This also adds a bit of flavour.

How to cook pasta

Pasta can be used in many ways. Stir some pesto through it and add peas for a quick dinner. Serve it with tomato sauce and vegetables or add meatballs. There are so many delicious things you can do with pasta that entire cookbooks have been written just about pasta!

In Italy, where pasta is very popular, cooks say that it should be cooked al dente. This means it still has a tiny bit that you can bite in the centre of each piece, so it's not completely soft and squishy.

About 75g of dried pasta is a good amount for each person (less for children).

1. To cook pasta, fill a large saucepan halfway with water, add a big pinch of salt to the water and put the lid on the pan.
2. Put the saucepan over a high heat on the hob to bring the water to a boil.
3. Remove the lid, then carefully add the pasta to the boiling water. Pasta likes lots of room as it cooks. It will swell up and get bigger, so don't fill the saucepan with too much pasta. Most dried pasta, either shapes or long strings like spaghetti, cooks in about 10 minutes – a minute longer for the fat shapes and a minute less for thin spaghetti. Check the packet to see what the recommended cooking time is.
4. Once the pasta has boiled for the right amount of time, drain it into a colander placed in the sink (ask an adult to help you do this).
5. It's now ready to be used however you like.

How to fry an egg

Fried eggs can be runny in the middle, sunny side up or flipped over at the end of cooking for over-well. Fried eggs are normally eaten for breakfast, but they are also good served on a bowl of noodles or with spicy fried rice.

1. Put a small splash of oil in a small frying pan over a medium heat. Swirl it around so the base of the pan is all lightly covered in oil. Put the pan on the hob and heat the oil until it's hot.

2. Gently crack your egg into a cup. If some shell cracks into it, fish it out with a spoon. Carefully pour the egg into the hot frying pan and wait while it cooks. The see-through part of the egg will quickly become white and the yellow yolk will begin to cook. Leave the egg to cook like this for sunny side up or flip it over so that the white and yolk cook on both sides.

3. The longer you leave the egg on the pan, the more the yolk will firm up. If you like the yolk runny, about 5 minutes will do (just make sure the white is completely cooked). For a well-done yolk, you will need to leave the egg on the pan for another 4 minutes. Use a fish slice to turn the egg and to take the egg out of the frying pan at the end, being careful of the hot oil.

How to boil an egg

1. Half-fill a saucepan with water. Put the pan on the hob on a high heat until the water is boiling.

2. Gently lower your egg into the water with a slotted spoon. Let it cook for 4 minutes for soft-boiled, 6 minutes for medium and 10 minutes for hard-boiled.

3. Carefully take the egg out of the water with the slotted spoon. Put it in a bowl of cold water and wait until it's cool enough to touch if you're peeling it for a salad or sandwich.

4. Pop a slice of bread in the toaster and spread butter on it while it's still warm, then slice it into soldiers to go with your egg.

How to make mashed potatoes

A chef's secret for making tasty mashed potatoes is butter – **lots** of butter. You can do this at home and make mash that tastes like it came from a restaurant.

There are lots of different varieties of potato. Each variety has a different name and has a different taste and texture. Some potatoes are fluffy when they are cooked, such as Maris Piper and King Edward. These will soak up lots of butter and milk when you mash them. Other potatoes are waxy and will make a creamier mash, such as new potatoes or varieties like Charlotte or Red Bliss.

1. Once you have chosen your variety of potato, wash them well and peel them.
2. If some potatoes are much bigger than others, cut the larger ones in half. You want all the potatoes to cook at the same time, so it helps if they are roughly the same size.
3. Put the potatoes in a large saucepan, cover the potatoes with water and put a lid on the pan. Put the pan on the hob on a high heat and bring the water to a boil. Turn the heat down and simmer the potatoes for about 25 minutes, until they are soft.
4. Drain the potatoes in a colander in the sink (ask an adult to help you do this). Let them sit in the colander for a minute or two to cool down.
5. Put the potatoes in a large bowl or the saucepan you cooked them in. Use a masher to mash them. This will take a little time, as you want to get rid of all the lumps.
6. For every 500g of potatoes, add 1 tablespoon of butter and 80ml milk to your mash (or use olive oil instead of butter if you prefer). Mash these in once the lumps are gone, then season with salt and pepper.
7. Leftover mashed potatoes can be used to make lots of things, such as carrot and potato cakes (see page 114), fish cakes, fritters or shepherd's pie.

Salad dressing

It's handy to have some salad dressing ready to go when you want to make a salad. This one has a nice sweet-and-sour taste because of the honey mixed with the vinegar and mustard.

Makes enough for 2 big salads

1 garlic clove
3 tablespoons olive oil
1 tablespoon apple cider vinegar
2 teaspoons mustard
2 teaspoons honey
salt and pepper

1. Peel and crush the garlic clove (see page 75 for instructions on how to crush garlic).
2. Put all the ingredients, including the crushed garlic, in a clean jam jar and put the lid on. Shake it all about, then drizzle the dressing over a salad.
3. This salad dressing will keep for a week in a sealed jar in the fridge if you want to make it ahead of time or if you have any left over.

Carrot top pesto

The lovely orange roots of the carrot plant are edible, but so are the leafy greens on top! Pesto is usually made with fresh basil, but this recipe uses those leaves.

Makes 1 jam jar

60g roasted unsalted cashew nuts
40g carrot top leaves
40g baby spinach
25g Parmesan cheese
120ml olive oil

1. Put the cashews, carrot top leaves and spinach in a blender or food processor.
2. Carefully cut the Parmesan cheese into four pieces, then put these in the blender or food processor too.
3. Pulse the blender or food processor to break everything down and mix them up. To pulse means turning the blender or food processor on and off about 10 times.
4. Turn off your blender or food processor. Use a spatula to scrape down the sides so everything is in the centre.
5. Turn the blender or food processor on the lowest setting. With the motor still running, slowly pour in the olive oil until everything is mixed together.
6. This pesto is delicious served on top of roasted vegetables or boiled potatoes. You can also dip bread into it or stir it through pasta. It will keep in an airtight jar in the fridge for a week.

Carrot and strawberry salad

Strawberries can be used in savoury food as well as desserts and this salad is a nice way to enjoy them for lunch or dinner. If you want to make the salad more filling, add some cubes of goat cheese or mozzarella.

Serves 4

1 carrot
2 handfuls of fresh strawberries
2 spring onions
2 large handfuls of salad leaves
1 sprig of fresh parsley
1 sprig of fresh oregano
1 sprig of fresh mint
3 tablespoons salad dressing (page 83)

1. Wash the carrot. Use a peeler to remove the carrot skin, then continue to peel the carrot into strips. Put the strips in a large bowl.
2. Chop the strawberries. Thinly slice the spring onions. Tear or chop the salad leaves and herbs. Add the strawberries, spring onions, salad leaves and herbs to the bowl with the carrots and toss together.
3. Pour the dressing over the salad and toss together.
4. Serve with crusty bread for a tasty summer lunch.

Kale, golden raisin and Parmesan salad

Black kale (also called cavolo nero) has dark green leaves with a thick stem going up the centre. Remove the stem before you cook it, as it's tough and difficult to eat. To do this, either use a knife and run it down each side of the stem or pull the leaf downwards. In this salad, the kale is sliced very thinly. These thin strips get nicely coated in dressing and grated cheese, giving them lots of flavour. It makes a nice lunch with some bread or is a good side dish for dinner.

Serves 6

250g black kale leaves, stalks removed
30g flaked almonds
125g Parmesan cheese
30g golden raisins
3 tablespoons salad dressing (page 83)

1. Pour some boiling water into a saucepan and add the kale leaves. Let them soak for 1 minute, then drain in a colander in the sink and allow to cool. Roll the leaves up into a sausage shape, then thinly slice the sausage so you get little strips of kale.
2. Spread the flaked almonds out in a big frying pan on a medium heat. Don't add any oil or butter – the nuts will toast in the hot, dry pan. Heat for about 4 minutes, until the almonds are just beginning to turn golden. Remove the pan from the heat and toss the almonds about in the pan for another minute. They will keep cooking on the still-warm pan but make sure they don't burn.
3. Grate the Parmesan on the thinnest side of a box grater.
4. Toss the kale with the toasted flaked almonds, the raisins and the salad dressing in a large bowl until everything is mixed well. Toss in the grated Parmesan and serve.

Broad bean and feta dip

In spring and summer, broad beans begin to ripen and swell inside their cosy pods. To cook them, gently twist the pod from the stalk of a bean plant, then pop the pod open to see a line of beans nestled inside a fluffy blanket. There is a thin skin on each bean but it's best to remove the skin before using the beans for this dip because it gives a smoother result. To remove the skin, pinch a bean between your fingertips and squeeze – the green bean should break through the white skin and push its way out. Broad beans can also be found in shops throughout the warmer months.

This dip can be eaten like hummus or guacamole. It's great with tortilla chips or spread on crackers. If you don't have broad beans, use peas instead.

Makes 1 bowl

225g broad beans, out of their pods and out of their shells
1 small garlic clove
50g feta cheese
1 tablespoon chopped fresh mint
1 teaspoon lemon juice
40ml light-coloured olive oil
salt and pepper

1. Before you boil your beans, get a bowl of very cold water ready to put the beans into after they are cooked. Add a few ice cubes to the water if you like.

2. Boil some water in a saucepan over a medium heat. Add your broad beans and boil the beans for 2 minutes.

3. Drain the beans in a colander in the sink, then put them into the cold water straight away. This is called blanching. It stops the beans cooking and it helps to keep their lovely bright green colour. Leave them for 1–2 minutes to get cold, then drain the cold water from the beans.

4. Peel and crush the garlic (see page 75 for instructions on how to crush garlic), then put it in a blender or food processor. Add the feta, mint, lemon juice and beans. Blitz on a low speed until it all starts to turn into a paste.

5. With the blender or food processor still running, slowly add the olive oil through the top. You want it to pour in an even stream, so having it in a small measuring jug works well. Turn off the blender or food processor and taste the dip. Add a little salt and pepper if needed. Feta can be quite salty so you may not need much salt.

6. The dip will stay fresh in the fridge for two or three days in an airtight container.

Herbs all taste different. If you're growing a selection of them, taste a few herbs at the same time so you can compare them and decide which ones you like best. This recipe uses mint but you could use chives or coriander for a different result.

Magic tomato sauce

This magic sauce is used in the next two recipes for patatas bravas and chilli. It can also be used for topping a pizza or tossing through pasta with grated cheese and some fresh basil.

Makes about 600ml

1 medium onion
1 small carrot
3 garlic cloves
1 tablespoon olive oil
1 x 400g tin of chopped tomatoes
1 tablespoon tomato purée
2 teaspoons honey or golden caster sugar
salt and pepper

1. Peel the onion and carrot, then chop them into small dice.
2. Peel and crush the garlic cloves using a garlic crusher (see page 75).
3. Pour the oil into a frying pan that has a lid. Put the pan on a medium heat on the hob. When the oil is hot, add the onion and carrot and sauté until the onion is see-through. This means keeping the temperature low and allowing the vegetables to cook slowly for 5 minutes. You can pop the lid on as they sauté – it will keep them moist. Just stir them every now and then.
4. Add the garlic and cook for about 3 minutes.
5. Stir in the tin of tomatoes, the tomato purée and the honey or sugar. Add 1 tablespoon of water to the empty tomato tin and swirl it around to rinse out the tin, then add the water to the pan. Season with salt and pepper to taste.
6. Put the lid back on the pan, reduce the heat to very low and allow the sauce to bubble for about 15 minutes.
7. Blitz the sauce with a soup gun or in a blender until smooth. It's now ready to use however you like.
8. Once the sauce has cooled completely, store it in the fridge. It will last for up to a week in an airtight container. If you would like to freeze some of your sauce to use later, it will last for up to a month in an airtight container or bag in your freezer.

> If you have a lot of fresh tomatoes, use them instead of a tin of tomatoes. About four or five ripe tomatoes weighing 500g and chopped up will do the trick.

Patatas bravas

Patatas bravas is a Spanish recipe. The smoked paprika, which is popular in Spain, gives the dish a smoky, spicy flavour. Waxy potatoes work best for this recipe because they keep their shape when you chop them into little cubes.

Serves 6

4 medium-sized waxy potatoes, such as Charlotte or Pink Fir Apple
1 tablespoon olive oil
a few sprigs of fresh thyme
a few sprigs of fresh rosemary
1 teaspoon smoked paprika
salt and pepper
4 tablespoons of the magic tomato sauce on page 86

1. Wash and peel the potatoes. Put them in a large saucepan and cover them with water. Cover the pan with a lid and put the pan on a high heat on the hob. Bring to a boil, then reduce the heat a little and cook for 15 minutes with the lid on.
2. Drain the potatoes in a colander in the sink and allow to cool. Once the potatoes are cool enough to touch, chop them into large dice.
3. Heat the olive oil in a saucepan over a medium heat on the hob. Add the potatoes. Cook for about 8 minutes, stirring occasionally, until they are golden brown all over.
4. Take the thyme and rosemary leaves off the stalks. You can throw away the stalks or add them to the compost bin.
5. Add the thyme, rosemary, smoked paprika and a pinch of salt and pepper to the potatoes. Cook gently for 3 minutes.
6. Gently heat your magic tomato sauce in a separate small saucepan on the hob.
7. Pour the warm sauce over the potatoes and stir to combine.
8. This will serve about six people or it can serve more if it's eaten as a side dish.

A big pot of chilli

This is a great family sharing dish. Put the pot in the centre of a table and allow everyone to help themselves. Three other bowls with rice, natural yogurt and chopped coriander can also be put on the table so people can add as much as they like.

Serves 6

1 small onion
1 small carrot
1 small stick of celery
1 small fresh chilli (or less if it's a very hot chilli) or 1 teaspoon mild chilli powder
1 x 400g tin of red kidney beans
1 tablespoon olive oil
½ teaspoon ground cinnamon

450g minced lamb or beef
salt and pepper
½ batch of magic tomato sauce (page 86)

To serve:
boiled rice
natural yogurt
fresh coriander

1. Carefully peel and chop your onion and carrot into very small square dice. Chop the celery stalk this way too.

2. Cut the chilli in half lengthwise, then scrape out the seeds and throw them away. Cut the red part of the chilli into thin strips. Extra care is needed for this, not just with the sharp knife, but with washing your hands after you chop the chilli. Chilli can really hurt your eyes or skin if you rub it in by accident after you touch one!

3. Open the tin of beans. Drain the beans in a colander in the sink to remove all the liquid, then rinse the beans. They are now ready to use.

4. Pour the oil into a large saucepan that has a lid. Put the pan over a low heat on the hob. When the oil is hot, add the onion and sauté until it's see-through. This means keeping the temperature low and allowing the onion to cook slowly for 5 minutes. You can pop the lid on as the onion sautés – it will keep it moist. Just stir every now and then.

5. Add the carrot and celery and sauté for another 5 minutes.

6. Add the chilli and cook for about 30 seconds, then stir in the cinnamon.

7. Add the mince to the pan and keep stirring until it's all browned. Break up any lumps with your wooden spoon as the mince is cooking.

8. Add the beans to your pan. Season with ½ teaspoon of salt and ¼ teaspoon of black pepper.

9. Add the magic tomato sauce and allow it to bubble away for about 30 minutes. Make sure the mince is cooked through by checking that all of the red or pink colour is gone.

...CONTINUED

10. Take a spoonful of the chilli and allow it to cool before tasting it. See if you think it needs a little more salt or pepper – this is called seasoning.
11. Serve your chilli with some boiled rice and a spoonful of natural yogurt on top. It's also good with some fresh coriander – just wash the leaves and stems, chop them up and sprinkle them over the top.

Dal

Dal comes from India and can sometimes be spelled dahl or dhal. It's a warm and comforting dish made with lentils and spices and is usually served with rice and naan.

Serves 6

1 small onion
1 small carrot
3 garlic cloves
1 teaspoon cumin seeds
½ teaspoon garam masala
¼ teaspoon ground turmeric

1 tablespoon rapeseed oil
200g ripe tomatoes, chopped
300ml vegetable or chicken stock
1 x 250ml tin of coconut milk
1 tablespoon tomato purée
150g dried red lentils
50g frozen or fresh peas
salt and pepper

1. Peel the onion and carrot, then chop them into small dice.
2. Peel and crush the garlic cloves (see page 75 for instructions on how to crush garlic).
3. Warm up a saucepan over a medium heat on the hob without any oil in it.
4. Put the cumin seeds, garam masala and turmeric in the warm, dry pan and toast them for less than 1 minute. This adds extra flavour and a nice nutty taste. Transfer to a plate and set aside – you'll add them to the dish later.
5. Add the oil to the pan, turn down the heat to low and let the oil heat up. Add the onion and sauté for 1 minute, then add the carrot. Sauté for about 6 minutes, until the onion is see-through. Add the garlic and cook for another 3 minutes.
6. Add the chopped tomatoes, stock, coconut milk and tomato purée. Stir well.
7. Add the lentils and the toasted spices that you set aside on the plate. Stir well again.
8. Put the lid on the pan and let it bubble away for about 15 minutes on a low heat, until the lentils are getting soft.
9. Add the peas and cook for another 5 minutes. Add a little water if the dal is getting too thick. Taste and season with a pinch of salt and pepper.
10. This is nice served with boiled rice and warm naan and a spoonful of natural yogurt on top. You can also sprinkle chopped fresh coriander or dried chilli flakes on top.

Rice paper rolls

These rolls are based on Vietnamese summer rolls. You can make lots of different dipping sauces, such as one with crushed peanuts or some sweet chilli sauce. The rice paper circles soften quickly when dipped in warm water, which makes them good for rolling. The aim is to make snug, sausage-shaped rolls packed with tasty ingredients.

Serves 6

- 50g thin rice noodles
- 8 lettuce leaves
- 20g fresh mint
- 20g fresh coriander
- 2 medium carrots
- 6 circular rice paper sheets (look for these where rice is sold in the shops or in an Asian market)

For the dipping sauce:

- 1 garlic clove
- 1 tablespoon soy sauce
- 1 tablespoon toasted sesame oil
- 1 teaspoon honey

1. Put the rice noodles in a pot. Boil some water in the kettle, then pour it over the noodles. Let them soak for 15 minutes – you don't need to keep the pot on the hob. Drain the noodles in a colander in the sink. Set aside.

2. Wash the lettuce, then tear the leaves into big pieces with your hands.

3. Wash and roughly chop the mint and coriander.

4. Peel the carrots, then cut them into thin ribbons with a peeler. To do this, put the carrot flat on a chopping board. Hold it at the top, then run the peeler down the length of the carrot. Repeat until you get to the inner core, which is lighter in colour. Flip the carrot over and repeat on the other side. You can eat the carrot cores as a little snack while you cook!

PEELING A CARROT into RIBBONS

5. Heat some more water in the kettle, then pour it into a large, shallow bowl, like a pasta bowl. When the water is cool enough that you can put your hand in it, dip one sheet of rice paper in the water for 10 to 15 seconds. Move it around until it's soft all over, then put it on a clean tea towel to dry.

6. Put the rice paper circle on a chopping board. Add some lettuce, mint, coriander, carrot ribbons and rice noodles close to the bottom edge of the circle. Lift the bottom of the roll over the filling and press it down, fold in the sides, then roll it up tightly into a sausage shape. Repeat with the other five rolls.

7. To make the dipping sauce, crush the garlic (see page 75). Mix the soy sauce, sesame oil, honey and crushed garlic in a small bowl or container.

8. To serve, dunk your roll in the dipping sauce and take a bite!

HOW TO MAKE the ROLLS:

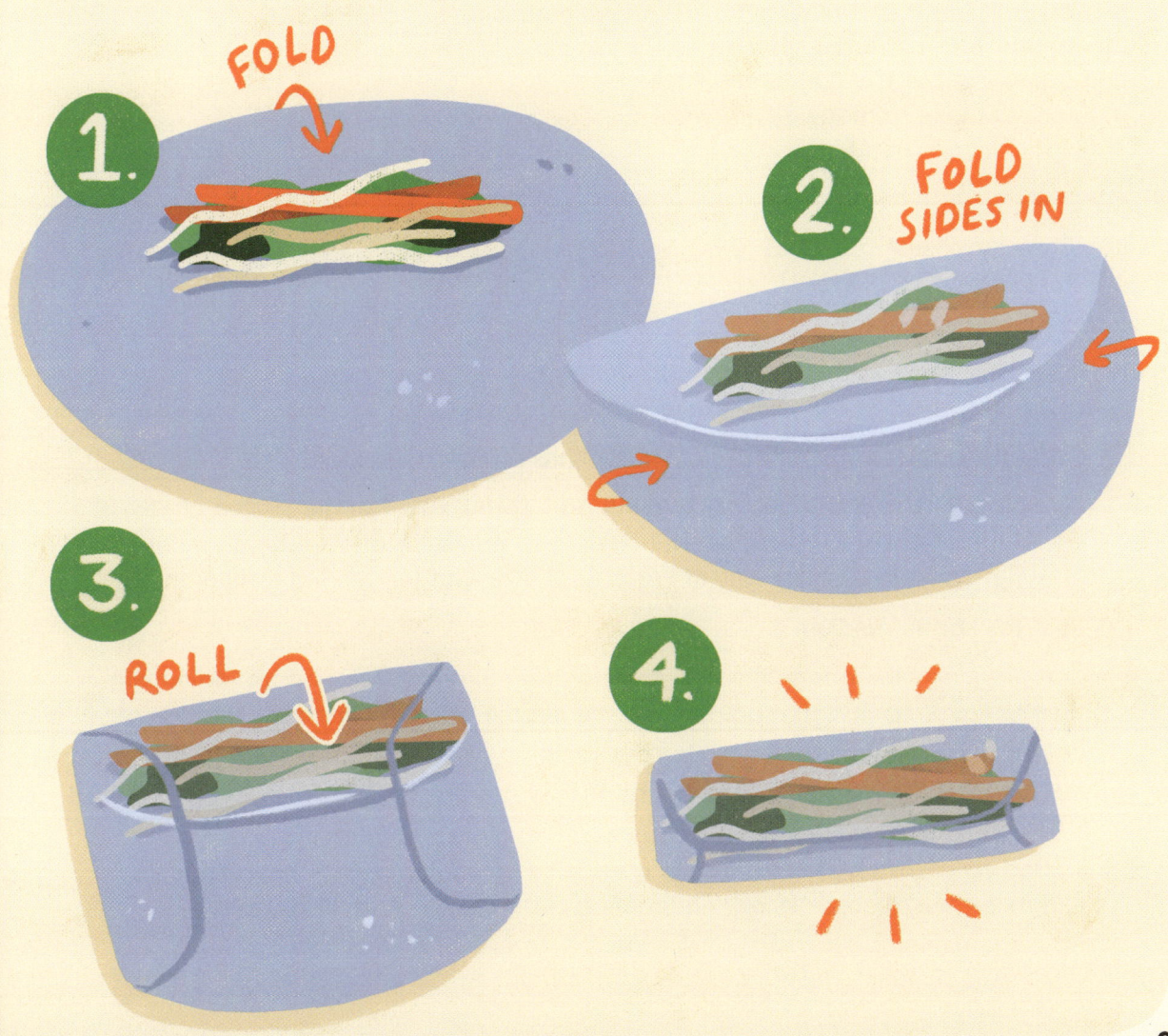

Cheese quesadilla

This is based on an old Mexican recipe. You can add different fillings, such as scrambled egg and guacamole, or add some hot sauce if you like spicy flavours. The tomato salsa on the next page is really nice spooned over the quesadillas. This recipe makes one quesadilla but you can multiply the amounts to make as many as you want.

Makes 1

80g Cheddar cheese
2 large tortillas
2 tablespoons sweetcorn
1 tablespoon tomato salsa (page 93)
a few sprigs of fresh coriander (optional)

1. Grate the cheese (see page 74 for instructions on how to grate).

2. Put one tortilla in a cold non-stick frying pan. Sprinkle half of the grated cheese all over the tortilla, then scatter over the sweetcorn, salsa and fresh coriander (if using). Sprinkle over the rest of the cheese, then put the second tortilla on top.

3. Heat the hob to medium.

4. Carefully carry the pan to the hob and put it on the heat. The bottom tortilla will start to warm up and turn golden and the cheese will start to melt. Use a fish slice to turn the quesadilla over so that the cheese on the other side melts and the other side of the quesadilla turns golden too. When it's done, slide it out of the pan onto a chopping board.

5. Melted cheese is very hot, so let the quesadilla sit on the chopping board for a minute or two to cool. Once it has cooled, cut it up into slices like a pizza.

Tomato salsa

You need to do quite a bit of chopping when making tomato salsa!

Serves 4

2 large ripe tomatoes
½ small red onion
½ fresh red chilli (or as much or as little as you like)
20g fresh coriander
1 lime
salt and pepper

1. Dice the tomatoes into small cubes. A small serrated knife works well for this.
2. Peel the red onion, then dice it up very small.
3. Use as much of the fresh chilli as you like. Taste a tiny bit of it before you add it to the salsa. Some chillies are really hot, so you will need less than others. Chop your chilli very finely. Wash your hands after you chop the chilli. Chilli can really hurt your eyes or skin if you rub it in by accident after you touch one!
4. Finely chop the coriander stalks and leaves.
5. Juice the lime.
6. Mix the chopped tomatoes, red onion, chilli and coriander together in a bowl, then season with a pinch of salt and pepper.
7. Add half of the lime juice and taste the salsa. Add more juice if you think it needs it.
8. There are lots of flavours involved in a salsa and it tastes even better when they can blend together for an hour or so at room temperature.
9. Serve your salsa with the quesadilla, with any type of eggs or with some roast chicken for dinner. Eat the salsa within two days of making it and keep it in the fridge in a jar.

Breakfast egg rolls

Rolling these up can be a little fiddly. The trick is to fold in both ends before you roll it up and then to roll it as tightly as possible. Use the more readily available flour tortillas or look for the corn variety. The corn ones give a nice flavour to the meal.

Makes 2

2 eggs
1 teaspoon hot sauce, such as Tabasco
a big pinch of salt
½ tablespoon sunflower oil
1 small ripe tomato

1 spring onion
a few sprigs of fresh coriander
100g Cheddar cheese
2 tortillas
½ lime, cut into two wedges

1. Crack the eggs into a small bowl. Add the hot sauce (or leave this out if you don't like spicy food) and a big pinch of salt and mix with a fork.

2. Turn the hob on to medium. Heat the oil in a frying pan, then pour the beaten eggs into the pan. Stir the eggs with a wooden spoon as they are cooking to scramble them. Leave them a little runny, as the eggs will continue to cook after you take the pan off the heat. Turn off the hob and leave the eggs in the pan while you do the next steps.

3. Carefully chop the tomato into small dice. Roughly chop the spring onion and coriander.

4. Grate the cheese (see page 74 for instructions on how to grate).

5. Preheat your oven to 200°C (180°C fan).

6. Put the tortillas on a baking tray. Pop them in the oven for about 5 minutes, until they are warm.

7. Flatten out one of the tortillas on a chopping board. Put half of the scrambled egg on one side of the tortilla. Sprinkle half of the chopped tomato over the egg, followed by half of the spring onion and coriander. Add half of the grated cheese and a squeeze of juice from one of the lime wedges.

8. Here comes the tricky part. Fold both ends of the tortilla inwards over the filling, then roll up the tortilla into a sausage shape. Roll it tightly so that the ingredients are nice and snug inside. It should look like a rectangular-shaped parcel. Do the same with the other tortilla and the rest of the ingredients.

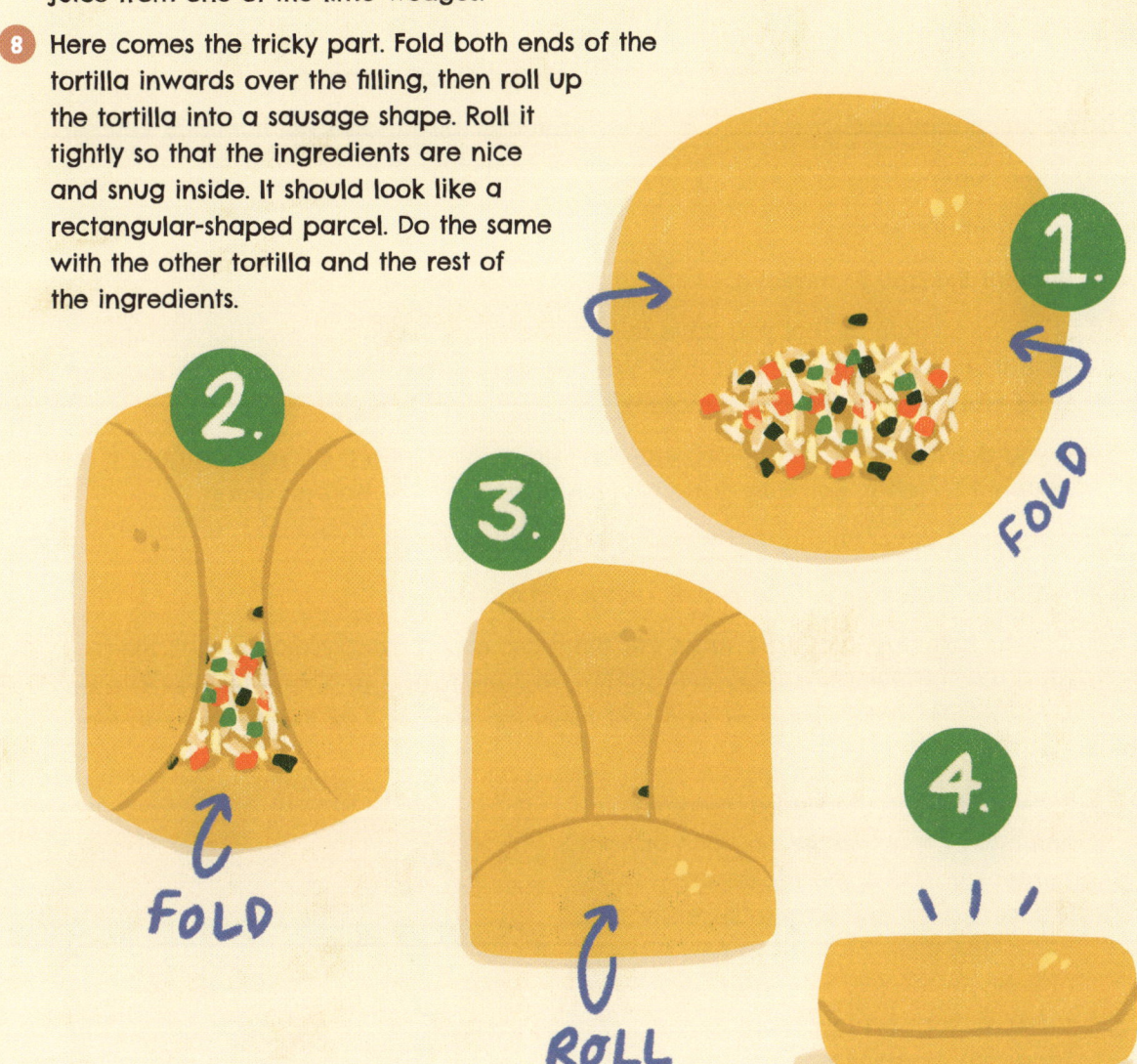

9. These make a great breakfast but can be eaten at any time of day.

Halloumi burgers

Halloumi is a squeaky cheese that comes in firm rectangular blocks. It comes from Cyprus and is traditionally made with sheep and goat milk, but nowadays it tends to have cow's milk added as well. Some people call it hellim, which is its Turkish name.

If you find halloumi to be a bit too salty, there are two things that you can do. The first is to pat the slices with kitchen paper before cooking them. If it's still too salty, soak the slices in a bowl of cold water for about 30 minutes, then pat them dry with kitchen paper or a clean tea towel. Patting them dry is important, because if you don't you won't get a nice crispy finish on the outside of the cheese.

Makes 4

1 ripe tomato

½ red onion (optional)

4 burger buns

rocket or lettuce leaves

450g halloumi cheese

tomato salsa (page 93), hummus, ketchup or mayonnaise

1. Preheat the grill to medium.
2. Slice the tomato so that you have four round slices. Tomatoes are more difficult to slice than you might think, as the knife can slip on the shiny skin. A small serrated knife works well for slicing tomatoes.
3. If you don't like raw red onion, you don't have to include it on your burgers. If you do want to use it, carefully cut eight thin slices from the half an onion.
4. Cut each burger bun in half if they are not cut already.
5. Wash the rocket or lettuce leaves and pat them dry.
6. Cut the halloumi into eight slices. Put the slices on a baking tray and grill them on a medium heat until they are golden. This will take 2 or 3 minutes. Use kitchen tongs to turn each slice over and grill them for another 2 or 3 minutes, until that side is golden too.
7. Spread some tomato salsa, hummus, ketchup or mayonnaise on each bottom burger bun. Put some rocket or lettuce leaves, one tomato slice and two onion slices on top. Put two slices of halloumi on top, then add some more rocket or a few more leaves. Sandwich together with the top burger bun and serve.

Pink coleslaw

This coleslaw can be served with the halloumi burgers. The red cabbage gives it a nice pink colour.

Makes 1 big bowl

2 small carrots
¼ small red cabbage
1 small spring onion
1 tablespoon mayonnaise
½ tablespoon natural yogurt
1 teaspoon mustard
1 teaspoon apple cider vinegar
¼ teaspoon cayenne pepper or ground black pepper
salt

1. Wash the carrots, then grate them with the large side of a box grater (see page 74 for instructions on how to grate).

2. Grate the red cabbage too. You should have equal amounts of grated carrots and cabbage.

3. Thinly slice the spring onion.

4. Mix the mayonnaise, yogurt, mustard, vinegar and pepper together in a large bowl. Add a few pinches of salt and mix everything together.

5. Put the grated carrot, grated cabbage and spring onion in the large bowl with the dressing. Using two forks, toss everything together until it's all mixed up.

6. Eat the coleslaw within a day of making it.

Sticky red onion and beetroot tart

You can buy nice buttery puff pastry in the freezer section of most supermarkets. It's a handy ingredient because it can be used in lots of different ways. Cut it into strips and roll them in some finely grated Parmesan, then after baking you have delicious cheese straws. Or cut puff pastry sheets into squares, put a quarter of a peach in the centre of each square, sprinkle with sugar and bake for a tasty treat. If you research puff pastry recipes, you will find lots more inspiration. This recipe uses red onions and beetroot to make a sweet and sticky tart filling.

Serves 4

1 large beetroot (about 300g)
1 medium red onion
3 tablespoons olive oil
2 tablespoons balsamic vinegar
2 tablespoons maple syrup

zest of 1 orange
¼ teaspoon ground cinnamon
salt and pepper
a little plain flour, for dusting
1 x 300g block of puff pastry, thawed

1. Preheat the oven to 200°C (180°C fan). Line a 23cm round tart tin with baking parchment.

2. Scrub the beetroot and cut it into thin wedges. Put the wedges in a baking dish.

3. Peel the red onion and cut it in half, then cut it into thin slices and put it in the dish with the beetroot.

4. Toss the beetroot and onion in the oil, vinegar, maple syrup, orange zest and cinnamon. Season with a little salt and pepper. Cover the dish with a lid or tin foil. Put the dish on the middle shelf of the preheated oven and bake for 40 minutes.

5. About half an hour after you put the vegetables in the oven, get your pastry base ready.

6. Lightly dust a clean countertop or a large chopping board with flour. Use a rolling pin to roll out your pastry if you have a block of it or unroll the sheet if that's what you are using.

7. Put a 25cm dinner plate upside down on top of the pastry. Using the plate as a guide, cut out a circle of pastry. Put this in the tart tin that you lined earlier. Pinch up the edges slightly so the circle fits neatly into the tin.

8. Let the beetroot and onion cool a little, then use a spatula to move all the ingredients to the centre of the pastry. If there is a lot of juice, leave some of it behind in the dish. Some beetroot are juicier than others. Spread out the filling in a single even layer but leave 2.5cm clear around the sides.

9. Put the tart in the oven and bake for 30 minutes, until the pastry is golden brown and the filling is sticky and bubbling slightly.

10. Allow the tart to cool in the tin, then gently remove it using the parchment paper. Cut the tart into slices to serve.

Rainbow wraps

Wraps can include lots of different ingredients, so choose what you like best. This recipe packs in all the colours of the rainbow.

Makes 2

¼ red pepper
½ small carrot
1 tablespoon sweetcorn or grated Cheddar cheese
roasted beetroot or pickled red onion

2 wraps
2 teaspoons mayonnaise
2 lettuce leaves or a few sprigs of fresh green herbs, such as basil or parsley
2 corn or wheat tortillas or wraps

1. Cut the red pepper into thin slices.
2. Grate the carrot (see page 74 for instructions on how to use a grater).
3. Grate the Cheddar cheese (if using).
4. Cut the roasted beetroot into thin slices (if using).
5. Lay one wrap out flat. Spread 1 teaspoon of mayonnaise all over it with a spoon.
6. To follow the rainbow, put the ingredients on the wrap in this order: red pepper, grated carrot, sweetcorn or grated cheese, lettuce or herbs, then finally the beetroot or pickled red onion. We are only missing something blue!
7. Roll the wrap up tightly. If you want to take it to school or somewhere else to eat later, wrap it up in some baking parchment or foil. Repeat with the remaining ingredients to make the second wrap.

Pumpkin and coconut soup

If you grow pumpkins, they are often all ready to be picked at the same time. Having some recipes to use them up is handy so they don't go to waste. This soup uses pumpkin, but you can also use leftover roasted vegetables like carrots or parsnips instead.

Serves 6

900g pumpkin flesh
1 onion
3 garlic cloves
a thumb-sized piece of fresh ginger
2 tablespoons olive oil
½ teaspoon mild chilli powder (optional)
400ml vegetable or chicken stock
1 x 400ml tin of coconut milk

1. Preheat the oven to 200°C (180°C fan).

2. Pumpkin is difficult to cut and to peel, as it can be quite hard. Ask an adult to help you cut it in half, take out the seeds from the centre, then peel it and cut it into large dice. Put these chunks in a roasting tin or a large ovenproof dish.

3. Peel the onion and cut it in half, then cut into thin slices. Add the onion to the roasting tin.

4. Crush the garlic with a garlic crusher (see page 75 for instructions on how to crush garlic) and add it to the roasting tin.

5. Grate the ginger (see page 74 for instructions on how to use a grater) and add it to the tin too.

6. Drizzle the oil and scatter the chilli powder (if using) over the pumpkin. Toss the pumpkin chunks to coat them in the oil.

7. Put the roasting tin in the oven. Roast the vegetables for about 30 minutes – the pumpkin should be soft after this time.

8. Remove the tin from the oven and allow everything to cool, then put all the vegetables in a big saucepan. Use the stock to rinse out the tin and add this to the saucepan too. Add the coconut milk.

9. Blitz the soup with a soup gun until it's smooth. Reheat gently until it's nice and warm, then ladle into bowls to serve.

Herby soda bread

Soda bread comes from Ireland and is a simple bread to make. Yeast, which is used for many other types of bread, needs time to rise. You also need to make sure it's at the right temperature as it rises. But when you make soda bread, you don't have to wait around beforehand. The raising agent is bread soda, which helps the bread rise during baking. By adding herbs from the garden to the dough, you can make a really good sandwich bread that is delicious with a slice of cheese.

Makes 1 loaf

450g plain white flour
1 level teaspoon bread soda
½ teaspoon salt
2 sprigs of fresh thyme
2 sprigs of fresh rosemary
1 egg
440ml buttermilk

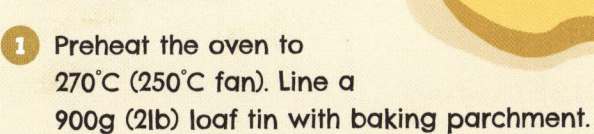

1. Preheat the oven to 270°C (250°C fan). Line a 900g (2lb) loaf tin with baking parchment.

2. Sieve the flour with the bread soda and salt into a big bowl.

3. Pull the little thyme leaves from the stalks (you can throw away the stalks or put them in the compost bin). Do the same with the rosemary. Chop the leaves roughly, then add them to the flour. Make a well in the centre.

4. In a jug, mix the egg and buttermilk together until they are combined. Pour this into the well in the flour. Mix with a wooden spoon until everything has come together and looks like a dough.

5. Scoop the dough into your lined loaf tin. Smooth the top with the back of a spoon, then make a line down the centre with a knife.

6. Put the tin on the middle shelf of your preheated oven and bake for 15 minutes. Turn down the oven temperature to 220°C (200°C fan) and bake for 30 minutes more.

7. Allow the bread to cool in the tin for about 10 minutes, until it's cool enough to handle. Carefully take the bread out of the tin and put it on a wire rack to cool completely.

Raspberry buns

You can make different versions of this bun recipe. You could use 50g of cocoa powder and 150g of self-raising flour to make chocolate raspberry buns. Or instead of adding raspberries, you could add the zest of two lemons to make lemon buns.

When you zest fruit, take off the thin colourful layer on the outside of the skin. Beneath this layer, the skin turns white – you don't want that white part, as it can be bitter. To zest fruit, use the smallest part of a box grater and gently rub it against the fruit.

Makes 12

4 eggs
½ teaspoon vanilla extract
200g butter, left out at room temperature until it's nice and soft
200g caster sugar
200g self-raising flour
50g fresh raspberries

1. Preheat your oven to 200°C (180°C fan). Pop 12 bun cases into a bun tray.
2. Mix the eggs and vanilla in a jug with a fork or whisk.
3. Put the soft butter and the sugar in a large mixing bowl. Using an electric mixer, beat the butter and sugar together for a few minutes, until the mixture is light and fluffy.
4. Slowly add the egg mixture to the butter mixture. If it starts to curdle (in other words, if the ingredients start to separate from each other), quickly add a small bit of the flour, then continue adding the eggs.
5. Add one-third of the flour at a time. Slowly mix it in before adding the next third.
6. Stop the mixer and scrape the sides of the bowl with a spatula a few times. This helps to completely combine the batter and stop any little volcano explosions happening in the buns!
7. Gently stir the raspberries through the batter.
8. Spoon the batter into the bun cases. Bake in the preheated oven for 15 minutes – the buns should look golden and have risen. When they are cool enough to handle, take them out of the tray and allow them to finish cooling on a wire rack.

Apple and blackberry crumble

This crumble uses blackberries that you can pick from the hedgerows at the end of the summer, but you can use another type of berry instead.

Serves 4

420g cooking apples (such as Bramley apples)
100g fresh blackberries
1 dessertspoon maple syrup
¼ teaspoon ground cinnamon
juice of ½ orange

For the crumble topping:

55g cold butter
85g plain flour
40g brown sugar
50g porridge oats

1. Preheat your oven to 200°C (180°C fan).
2. First, make the crumble topping. Cut the butter into small cubes.
3. Mix the flour and sugar together in a large bowl, then add the cubes of butter. Start to rub the butter, flour and sugar between your palms. The aim is to combine them all so the mixture looks like breadcrumbs. It will take a minute or two. You shouldn't see any big chunks of butter when you're done.
4. Stir in the porridge oats and set the bowl aside.
5. Peel the apples, cut them in half and cut the cores out of the centres. Cut the apples into large dice.
6. Use a baking dish that can go into a hot oven and that the crumble ingredients will fit into. Put half of the apples and half of the blackberries in the dish. Pour over the maple syrup and sprinkle with half of the cinnamon.
7. Add the rest of the apples and blackberries. Pour over the orange juice.
8. Sprinkle the crumble over the top so that the apples and blackberries are all covered. Press it down lightly, then sprinkle on the rest of the cinnamon.
9. Bake in the preheated oven for about 30 minutes. Push a butter knife into the centre to make sure all the apple chunks are soft.
10. Let the crumble cool for about 15 minutes before serving. This is nice with custard, cream or ice cream.

Homemade yogurt

You can make lots of different foods from milk: yogurt, cheese, cream, butter, crème fraîche, ice cream. These foods were created to make milk last longer and they taste great too. Turning milk into yogurt not only adds bacteria to help your gut and tummy stay happy, it will also last for over a week in the fridge.

Makes about 800ml

950ml full-fat milk
2 tablespoons cream
2 tablespoons natural yogurt with live bacteria

1. Put the milk and cream in a saucepan set over a low heat. Heat just until they are beginning to shiver, before they boil. The surface will start to wobble and the first little bubbles will appear at the edge.

2. Take the saucepan off the heat. Let the milk cool down to a warm body temperature. This means that it feels nice and warm if you touch it, but not hot.

3. Use a small clean cup to scoop about 125ml of the milk into another bowl. Mix the yogurt into this cup of warm milk in the second bowl until it's smooth. Stir this back into the main saucepan of milk with a wooden spoon.

4. Put a lid on the saucepan and leave it in a warm place for 8 to 12 hours. A hot press or on top of a fridge might do. You can wrap the saucepan in some towels to keep it cosy or even sit it on a hot water bottle.

5. The yogurt should be thick and creamy after 12 hours. You can now put it in an airtight container in the fridge to cool before eating it. It will keep in the fridge for up to 10 days.

Strawberry yogurt pops

You will need ice pop moulds to make these. These moulds come in different sizes, so you might need to use a little more or a little less of the mixture to fill yours. These are lovely made with banana or mango as well.

Makes 4 small pops

4 big juicy strawberries
4 tablespoons natural yogurt

1. Mash the strawberries into a mush, then mix this with the yogurt. It might take a little practice to spoon the mixture into the moulds and put the tops on.

2. The pops will need at least 3 hours in the freezer to firm up. Run warm water over the moulds to help you take the pops out when you're ready to eat them.

Mint lemonade

This is a refreshing, tasty drink on a summer day. It's perfect for a picnic and can even be used for a lemonade stand.

Serves 2

2 tablespoons caster sugar
150ml hot water
3 sprigs of fresh mint
2 lemons
ice cubes

1. Stir the sugar into the hot water in a mug until it dissolves, then add the mint leaves. Now muddle the mint into the sugar and water – this means using the back of a wooden spoon to bash it all up a bit.

2. Let the mint sit in the water for about 30 minutes, then strain the mixture through a sieve. You can throw away the mint now or put it in the compost bin.

3. Carefully cut the lemons in half and squeeze them.

4. Put some ice cubes in two glasses. Pour the lemon juice and the mint syrup over the ice, then top up the glasses with cold water. Give them a stir before serving.

REUSING

What is a circular food system?

There is no waste in nature – everything is reused. When a leaf falls off a tree, it's eaten by bugs. Whatever remains rots into the ground to make the soil richer for growing plants the following season.

A circular food system would work a bit like this. If food is not going to be eaten, it could go to someone else who will eat it. Or people could collect the food and feed it to farm animals instead of throwing it into the bin. Leftover food could also be used to make compost to grow more food. Used coffee grinds could even be used to make a new coffee cup!

There are lots of clever, circular ways that we can make sure food waste is not waste at all, but instead is something valuable for our food system.

Food waste

About one-third of all the food in the world is wasted. Some food is lost on farms and in factories. Other food gets damaged when it's sent on long journeys to supermarkets or shops. Shops cause food waste as well – fruit or vegetables can get bruised or they might not be stored properly.

Sometimes people buy too much food or don't use food in time, which also leads to food waste. Forgetting to eat leftovers is one of the biggest reasons that food is wasted in a home, so having a few ideas of how to use your leftovers can help to reduce the amount of food that gets thrown away. See pages 114–117 for recipes and ideas.

Environmental impact

When food is wasted in shops or in homes, all the energy that was used to make the food and to transport the food to those places is wasted. The packaging the food is in also gets thrown out. These things create the carbon footprint of food. The carbon used and wasted at each different stage causes greenhouse gas emissions, which in turn are causing climate change.

Refrigeration

There are lots of ancient ways to store food. Some of these are still useful today, while others are not so popular anymore.

Using a fridge is the most common way to help food last longer and stay fresh at home. The cold air inside the fridge helps to stop the food going off or spoiling.

Before people had fridges, they had to buy or make their food fresh each day or else find ways to make it last longer. Nooks, which are little holes in walls, were used to keep things cool. Storing food in colder parts of buildings, such as a basement or cellar, was also popular. Food was usually put in wooden or clay containers before being stored in a cool, dark basement. Special cooling houses were built in some villages to keep people's meat, fruit and vegetables stored safely.

Airtight containers

Airtight containers help to preserve food that doesn't need to be kept in the fridge. The containers do this by keeping air away from the food. They also stop foods from drying out and prevent any extra water from getting in.

Bog butter

In areas where the land was soft and boggy, people dug holes in the bog and buried butter inside wooden barrels to keep it cool. Butter that was more than **3,500 years old** has been found like this in bogs and it was still okay to eat!

IT'S STILL OKAY TO EAT!

YOU GO FIRST.

Why do we freeze food?

In very cold countries, people freeze food, such as seal meat, on the ice. In other places, people use freezers to keep food for longer.

Most foods have some water inside them. For example, a potato is 79% water. Microbes and bacteria react with this water to turn the food sour or rotten. When you freeze food, it is stored at such a low temperature that the microbes and bacteria can't make the food go bad because the water has turned into solid ice crystals.

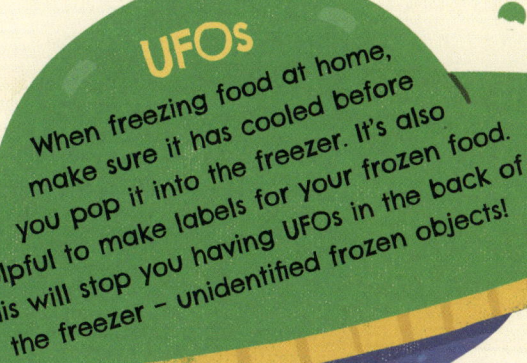

UFOs
When freezing food at home, make sure it has cooled before you pop it into the freezer. It's also helpful to make labels for your frozen food. This will stop you having UFOs in the back of the freezer – unidentified frozen objects!

Tinned food

Canning food or sealing it inside jars was invented to help feed soldiers on the battlefield. Napoleon, who was the ruler of France in the 1800s, wanted to get food to his army and navy, which were spread out across Europe. He needed to make sure the food didn't go off on the journey, so he ran a competition with a prize for the person who invented the best way to do this. A man called Nicolas Appert heated the food and sealed it inside airtight jars. He won the prize of 12,000 francs, which was a lot of money at the time. This way of making food last is still used today, but now tin cans are the most popular way to seal the food.

The tin opener was invented **50 years** after businesses started using tin cans to seal food. Before it was invented, people used hammers and chisels to get their food out of the can!

Salting meat and fish

Food can be preserved in many ways. Hanging meat or fish to dry it out or curing it with salt both make it last longer. Sometimes the two methods are used together.

Salt takes water out of the meat or fish so that the microbes and bacteria that make it go off can't damage it. This way of preserving food not only makes the food last longer, but it also adds flavour to it.

Bacon and ham start out as pork and then have salt added to them. In Spain, legs of salted pork are hung up to dry, then thinly sliced and eaten cold. Fish such as cod or salmon can also be dried and salted.

HAVE YOU BEEN OUT HERE FOR A WHILE?

YES, WHY DO YOU ASK?

Drying fruit and vegetables

In ancient times, people in hot climates dried foods in the sun or in the wind, which removed the water from the food and helped it to last longer. Drying fruit and vegetables is still popular. Prunes, raisins, dried apricots, sun-dried tomatoes and chillies have all been dried. Taking the moisture out of them not only helps them last longer because it stops them from getting rotten, but it can also make the flavour stronger, turning them into quite different ingredients from how they started out. For example, when you dry a grape it turns into a raisin and the flavour changes completely.

Pickling

Pickling means soaking food in vinegar. Fruit and vegetables are usually covered in hot vinegar and put inside a jar with a tight lid to keep the air out. Pickles have a tangy taste because of the vinegar, which also helps the food to last quite a long time.

Fermenting

Fruit and vegetables that are sprinkled with salt and allowed to sit until they begin to change flavour are called fermented. Fermented foods are often good for us because they put nice friendly bacteria into our guts, which help us to stay healthy and happy.

The earliest record of pickling goes all the way back to 4000 BCE in India.

Preserving food allowed people to travel further from home. The food could be stored in small amounts and carried on long journeys without going bad.

Sugaring

Sugaring is when food is covered in honey or sugar to keep air away from it and to help it last longer. The sugar takes the water out of the food and sweetens it at the same time. In ancient Greece and Rome, people started mixing hot sugar and fruit together and invented jam.

Making milk last longer

Milk can be turned into cheese, which helps it to last for years. Some Italian Parmesan cheeses are decades old!

Making yogurt is another way to make milk last longer. It also gives us interesting new tastes. You can make your own homemade yogurt using the recipe on page 104.

Butter is the cream from milk that has been churned and preserved with salt. Churning means shaking or whisking the cream until it separates into firm butter and liquid buttermilk. See page 118 for instructions on how to make your own butter.

A VERY OLD CHEESE

Reviving food

Limp or wilted vegetables, lettuce leaves or herbs can be revived in cold water. The little cells in the vegetable or leaves begin to absorb water and swell. This plumps them up and refreshes them, which makes them tastier to eat.

Magic lettuce hearts

The tightly closed leaves at the centre of a head of lettuce are called the heart. If you put the bottom of the heart of lettuce in some water, it will grow into another head of lettuce!

To try this, put the heart in a glass of water that has about 2cm of water in it. Sit this on a sunny windowsill and change the water every two days. After about 12 days, new leaves will have grown and you will have a brand-new head of lettuce.

Stale bread

If bread is a day or two old, it goes hard and is called stale bread. It may not taste very good on its own, but it can be used in lots of different ways.

Stale bread is great for making toast. Or it can be popped in the freezer, already sliced, then put straight into your toaster when you need it.

Put stale bread in a blender and blitz it up to make breadcrumbs.

Cut a slice of stale bread into small squares. Put the squares on a baking tray and toss in some oil and salt and pepper, then bake in an oven preheated to 200°C (180°C fan) until golden. After cooling, you have croutons that can be added to soups and salads.

Stale bread is often used in recipes like bread and butter pudding or eggy bread (page 115).

Cut-and-come-again green leaves

You can cut leaves from leafy green plants like lettuce, kale and chard, then come back and pick the leaves again another day.

If you're growing broccoli, beetroot, carrots or cauliflower, you can also eat the green leaves from the plant.

Potato peels

If you have some clean potato peels, put them on a baking tray, toss them in some oil and salt and pepper, and bake them in an oven preheated to 200°C (180°C fan) until they are nice and crisp. Add some grated cheese when they come out of the oven for a great snack.

Leftovers recipes
Carrot and potato cakes

Makes 6 small cakes

2 tablespoons leftover or cooked, mashed carrots
3 tablespoons mashed potatoes
½ tablespoon plain flour
½ teaspoon ground nutmeg
¼ teaspoon smoked paprika
salt and pepper
1 egg
1 small spring onion
1 tablespoon olive or sunflower oil

1. If you have leftover boiled, steamed or roasted carrots, just mash them up.
2. Put the mashed carrots and mashed potatoes in a large bowl and mix them together. Add the flour, nutmeg and smoked paprika, then season by adding a pinch of salt and a pinch of ground black pepper to the bowl. Stir together.
3. Crack the egg into the bowl.
4. Before chopping the spring onion (some people call them scallions), cut off the white tip with the little roots and the ends of the green tops. Chop the rest of the spring onion really small. Add this to the other ingredients in the bowl and stir everything together.
5. Put the oil in a frying pan and put the pan on a medium heat on the hob. Drop a big spoonful of the mixture into the pan and spread it out slightly with the back of the spoon. Allow it to cook for about 2 minutes, until the bottom is golden. Use a fish slice to carefully turn it over and cook for another 2 minutes, until that side is golden too. Repeat with the rest of the mixture to make six small cakes.
6. These are nice served with relish or chutney, or sour cream mixed with chopped chives and black pepper.

Eggy bread and hot fruit

Serves 4

2 eggs
120ml milk
1 teaspoon ground cinnamon
1 teaspoon vanilla extract
4 thick slices of stale bread
1 tablespoon sunflower oil or soft butter

For the hot fruit:

zest of 2 oranges
250g fresh or frozen berries
1 tablespoon caster sugar
1 tablespoon honey

1. Mix the eggs, milk, cinnamon and vanilla in a wide baking dish that will fit at least two slices of bread at a time. Soak all four slices. You want the liquid to really soak into the bread so it becomes nice and squishy. The slices will become more difficult to move once they have been soaked.

2. Heat the butter or oil in a big frying pan set over a medium heat on the hob. Use a fish slice to move each slice of bread from the dish to the pan. Cook the soaked bread until it's golden brown on the bottom, then turn each slice over and cook until that side is golden brown too.

3. The hot fruit is a good way to use up berries that are becoming too soft. If it's a time of year when there aren't many fresh berries, use frozen ones instead – just cook them for about 4 minutes longer.

4. Grate the zest from the oranges using the smaller holes of a box grater (see page 74 for instructions on how to use a grater). Try not to use any of the white part of the zest, as it can be quite bitter.

5. Put the orange zest, berries, sugar and honey in a saucepan and put it on the hob over a medium heat. Allow it to gently bubble away for about 6 minutes (or for 10 minutes if you're using frozen berries). Take the pan off the heat and allow to cool, then taste it. If it's a little too sour, stir in a teaspoon of honey.

6. To serve, put one slice of eggy bread on a plate, then spoon some of the hot fruit on top. A big spoonful of natural yogurt is nice with it too.

Leftover vegetable buns

Makes 12

80g leftover cheese
200g self-raising flour
3 eggs
100ml light-coloured olive oil

100ml milk
1 tablespoon tomato purée
3 pinches of salt
150g leftover cooked vegetables

1. Preheat the oven to 200°C (180°C fan).
2. Pop 12 bun cases into a bun tin.
3. Use whatever leftover cheese that you like. A hard cheese like Cheddar is handy for grating, while a soft cheese like goat cheese can be crumbled. If you have a hard cheese, grate it using a box grater (see page 74 for instructions). Having a big piece of cheese to grate stops your hands from being too close to the sharp part of the grater. It can be easier to weigh the cheese after it's grated.
4. Sieve the flour into a large bowl.
5. Crack the eggs into a separate large bowl. Add the oil, milk, tomato purée and salt. Stir until they are all mixed together.
6. You can use leftover steamed, boiled or roasted vegetables, but they need to be mashed up before you add them to the other ingredients. You can use a mixture of any vegetables that you have left over – a mixture of carrots and courgettes with peas or parsnips is good.
7. Add the wet ingredients to the flour. Add the vegetables too. Stir everything together.
8. Scoop the mixture into your lined bun tin. Put the tin in the preheated oven and bake for about 25 minutes, until the buns have risen and are golden brown.
9. Put the tin on a wire rack to cool.
10. These are great as a snack or packed into a school lunchbox.

Chicken stock

Stock is a great way to get extra use out of a chicken dinner. You can also use vegetables that are going a bit limp, which means they aren't very fresh. You might not want to eat them in a salad, but they are okay for making stock, as they are just used to flavour it and give it some extra goodness.

You can make beef stock, fish stock or vegetable stock if you don't have a leftover chicken. They can all be made the same way, just using a different main ingredient.

Makes 750ml

1 onion
1 carrot
1 leek
all the bones and any leftovers from a roast chicken
a handful of fresh rosemary
a handful of fresh thyme
1.5 litres water

1. Peel the onion and cut it into four pieces. Cut the carrot and leek into four pieces too.

2. Put all the ingredients in a big pot with a lid. Put the pot on the hob over a high heat. Bring it to a boil, then reduce the heat to low so that it simmers for 2 hours. Turn off the heat and allow it to cool for 30 minutes.

3. Put a big bowl under a colander. Carefully pour everything from the pot into the colander. The stock will drip through to the bowl beneath. Throw out the bits left behind in the colander.

4. The stock will last in the fridge for a week in a clean airtight container. You can also freeze the stock for later – it will last for two months in the freezer.

Activity: Shake it all about butter

You will need:
- A clean jar with a tight-fitting lid
- Some fresh cream at room temperature

1. Half-fill a clean jar with room-temperature cream. Put a tight-fitting lid on the jar.

2. Shake the jar all about! The cream will start to change. After a minute or so, it won't be liquid anymore – it will be whipped cream.

3. After even more shaking, the whipped cream will start to separate. There will be a yellow lump and some liquid. The lump is butter and the white liquid is buttermilk. This buttermilk is good for baking bread or scones, so don't throw it away!

4. Scoop the butter from the jar. You can now eat it on bread or toast. No salt has been added to it, so you might find that it tastes different to most butter that you buy in the shops. Add some salt if you like.

5. Wrap your butter snugly in baking parchment or put it in an airtight container. It will will keep in the fridge for three or four days.

Activity: Make plastic out of milk

You will need:
- A small saucepan (or a microwave)
- A cup of leftover milk
- 4 teaspoons distilled white vinegar
- A mug
- A clean tea towel
- A rolling pin or cookie cutter (optional)

If you have some leftover milk, you can use it to make plastic! It's not as strange as it sounds – milk was used to make buttons, pens, beads and jewellery from 1900 to about 1945. It's called casein plastic. Casein is found in milk. It's a protein that gives milk its white colour. Tiny casein molecules can stick to one another to form a natural plastic.

1. Use a small saucepan on the a hob or a microwave to heat a cup of milk until just before it boils – it should be shivering on the top.

2. Add 4 teaspoons of distilled white vinegar to a mug, then pour the hot milk on top of it. The milk will begin to separate. The lumps are called curds. Stir the contents of the cup to break up the curds.

3. Put a clean tea towel on a table or countertop. Scoop the curds from the cup onto the towel and pat them dry. Form them into a ball.

4. Knead the ball by pushing and pulling it like you do when you are making yeast bread.

5. Form your plastic into a shape or roll it with a rolling pin and cut it with a cookie cutter. It will harden overnight.

EATING

Eating with other people makes us happy

It's nice to eat with other people. Most people are sociable and like to chat and tell each other stories. This relaxes us, which helps us to absorb the food and let it digest in our tummy. Scientists have found that eating with other people releases endorphins, which are chemicals in our body that make us happy.

Eating with other people helps us connect

In every culture, people eat together. From ancient tribes and big medieval banquets for kings and queens to your own kitchen table at home, sharing food connects people with each other.

Even if people speak a different language, they can still eat together and enjoy the same foods and smile happily when they think something tastes good. Eating together helps us to connect with other people and build a community because it helps us to see what we have in common. Eating together can also create nice memories.

Sharing food to show your love

A lot of love can go into making and serving food. Sharing food with people can show you care about them. If a friend is unwell, it can be nice to call with a slice of cake or some fruit to cheer them up.

In most parts of the world, families use food to welcome someone into their home. It's a way to show friendship. It also helps to keep traditions and old recipes alive when people who have moved away proudly cook special dishes from their own country.

Eating a rainbow

Food is the fuel that gives you the energy to run, play and think. Vitamins and nutrients in food help you to grow and can protect you from getting sick. Eating lots of different, wholesome foods gives you the energy that you need. By eating a rainbow of fruits and vegetables, you get variety in your diet. Including one colourful fruit or vegetable a day is a good way to start.

Your gut-brain axis

After you eat food, it passes through the gut. Your gut is made up of about 5 metres of intestines as well as your stomach. Your gut is linked to your brain, so a happy gut can make you happy.

Drinking water and exercising help food to move through your digestive system. Friendly bacteria help to break the food down. Eating lots of different fruit, vegetables, grains and nuts helps to keep these bacteria working properly. Yogurt and fermented foods like kimchi and sauerkraut help too.

Smells so good

Your body reacts to the smell of delicious food when it's cooking or is on your plate. It signals that you should eat the food by making your mouth water. It does that by releasing saliva in your mouth and fluid in your gut to get your appetite going.

Fibre

There are foods that we can't fully digest, but it's still good to have them in our diet. These foods have fibre in them, which is important to keep food moving through your body and to help you adsorb nutrients and other important things. Foods like beans, apples and broccoli give you fibre.

Connecting cultures

There are so many different foods from around the world, it would be impossible to even imagine them all. But when you look closely, you can see connections between different countries and different foods. For example, tomatoes were grown by the Aztecs in Mexico and then shipped to Italy. Now it's hard to imagine Italian food without tomatoes because they are so important for making pizza and pasta sauces. Potatoes are popular in Ireland, but they came from Peru. Apple pie is popular in the United States, but all the ingredients were brought to that country from other places. The apples originally came from Central Asia, the flour came from the Middle East and the sugar came from South-East Asia.

Companion

The word 'companion' means 'friend'. It's someone you like being with and who makes you feel relaxed. The old meaning for the word in Latin and French means 'with bread', or sharing bread with someone. Sharing bread is important in lots of different cultures. Almost every country in the world has some type of bread that is special to them. In Ireland it's soda bread, in India it's naan and in France it's a baguette. Sharing bread with someone can be a sign of friendship and make you their companion.

Eating utensils

While people all around the world share meals together, they do it in different ways. In some countries people sit on mats on the floor, while others sit on chairs at a table. In many places, people eat using their hands or they use bits of bread to scoop up their food. In countries like China, Japan, Korea and Vietnam, people eat with chopsticks. In most parts of Europe and North America, people use knives and forks. Spoons are used all over the world.

Food customs and table manners

We learn from older people like relatives and from our friends about how to eat certain things, how to share our food and how to chat and talk about things during a meal. In Spain, when people relax and sit around a table after they finish eating a meal, they call it sobremesa.

Different people have different ways of doing things. These are often called food customs or table manners. In South Korea, for example, people think it's nice to wait for the oldest person at the table to take the first bite. Once the oldest person has started to eat, you can too.

Celebrations

Food is used to celebrate important times in people's lives. It's also used during festivals throughout the year. Cakes are important for birthdays and weddings. Pumpkins are used at Halloween. Hot chocolate is made for Día de los Muertos (Day of the Dead) in Mexico. Toshikoshi soba (buckwheat noodles) are served for the New Year in Japan.

Activity: Spill the beans and share the love

1. Talk to someone who is older than you, such as an older relative or someone in your neighbourhood. Ask them about the meals they ate when they were a child. Ask them about an interesting or tasty meal that they remember well.

2. Working with an adult, try to recreate that meal for them. You might need to use your detective skills to look for recipes and ingredients.

3. Once you have organised the ingredients and cooked the dishes for the meal, make a table plan. A table plan is a drawing of how you are going to serve your memorable meal. Think of what you want to serve the food on – would large plates in the middle of the table work well so that everyone can help themselves? Or will you give everyone their own plate? There are a lot of decisions to make when setting your table, but things don't need to be perfect. The main thing is that people have fun and enjoy each other's company.

Activity: Write a story or poem

Write a story or poem that ends with the line:

and this is how food brings people together.

Think of all the ways we share meals, how people all over the world use food to celebrate important things like weddings or birthdays, or how food is used to show you care about someone.

INDEX

Activities are shown in **bold**.

airtight containers 108
animals, pollination by 6, 26
annual plants 40
antibiotics 17
ants 26
Appert, Nicolas 109
apple and blackberry crumble 103
asparagus 40

bacteria 15–17, 19, 104, 109–11, 121
bats 26
bean pods 7
beans 7, 11–12, 18
beef 62
beehives 29
bees 24–6 see also bumblebees, honeybees
beet family 43
beetles 26
beetroot and red onion tart 98
biodiversity 8
birds 27
bitter (taste) 53
bog butter 108
bread 122
  eggy 115
  stale 113
breakfast egg rolls 94–5
broad bean and feta dip 85
build a bug house 30
bumblebees 26, 29
butter 111
  making 118
butterflies 27
buying food 60–9

cabbage family 43
canned food 109

carbon footprint 107
carrots 8, 40, 48, 83
  carrot and potato cakes 114
  carrot and strawberry salad 84
  carrot family 43
  carrot top pesto 83
  carrot tops 48, 83
casein plastic 119
cavolo nero 84
celebrations 123
cereals 19
cheese 111
cheese quesadilla 92
chicken stock 117
chilli 88–9
chitting potatoes 37
chopping 76
climate 38
climate change 38, 107
clover 18
cocoa beans 62
coffee grounds 36
coleslaw, pink 97
colour psychology 66
comfort foods 57
compost 36, 64
cooking 70–105
courgettes 37, 47
cows 62
crop rotation 18, 42
crumble, apple and blackberry 103
cucumber family 43
curing food 110
cut-and-come-again plants 113

dal 89
dopamine 57
drying food 110

earthworms 16–17
eating 120–4
eating a rainbow 121
eating together 120
eating utensils 122
egg rolls 94–5
eggs, cooking 81
eggshells 36
eggy bread 115
epiphytic plants 20

farming 38, 62
fermented food 111, 121
fertilizers 18–19, 62
fibre 121
find a rainbow 51
flavour 55
flavourists 55
flies 27
food advertising 66
food colours 57
food cultures 122
food customs 123
food leftovers 107
food memories 57, 71
food miles 49, 63
food miles detective 69
food packaging 64, 66
food system 60–1
  circular 106
food waste 106–7
framing nature 21
freezing food 109
fruit trees 35
fruits, definition 7

garlic, crushing 75
genes 8
genetic editing 9
genetic modification (GMO foods) 9
glasshouses 39
gluts 49

grating 74
gravitational pull 38
greenhouse gases 62, 107
grow a seedling 12–13
growing food 32–42
gut–brain axis 121

Haber–Bosch process 19
halloumi burgers 96
herbs 31, 50, 78
herby soda bread 101
honey 28
honeybees 28
honeyeater 27
hoverflies 25
how meals connect us 68
hummingbirds 27
hydroponics 9

industrial foods 65
insects 12, 24–6
  as food 71
intensive farming 19
International Space Station 9

jam 111

kale, golden raisin and Parmesan salad 84
kitchen equipment 72–3
kitchen safety 73
kitchen skills 74–9

ladybirds 26, 37
leafy vegetables 48
leftover vegetable buns 116
leftovers 107, 114–17
legumes 7 see also beans, peas

125

lemonade, mint 105
lettuce
  family 43
  reviving 112
light pollution 25

McLean, Malcolm 65
magic tomato sauce 86
making plastic out of milk 119
methane 62
microbes 109–10
milk 111, 119
mini polytunnel 41
mint lemonade 105
mirepoix 77
moths 27
mouthfeel 56
mycelium 20

Napoleon Bonaparte 109
nectar 24
nutrients 10
nuts 7

onion family 43
organic farming 62

pasta, cooking 80
patatas bravas 87
peas 7, 11–12, 18, 48
  pea/bean family 7, 43
  pea pods 7
peanuts 7
peeling 75
perennial plants 40
pesticides 25, 37
pesto, carrot top 83
pH 22–3
pick a pizza 51
picking food crops 44–7
pickling food 111
pink coleslaw 97
planting times 34–5

plastic, casein 119
pollen 24, 29
pollination 24–31
pollinator pot 31
polytunnels 39, 41
potatoes 37, 122
  chitting 37
  mashed 82
  potato and carrot cakes 114
  potato family 43
  potato peels 113
preserving food 108–11
pumpkin and coconut soup 100
pumpkins 37

quadrat 21
quesadilla 92

rainbow wraps 99
raspberry buns 102
recycling 64
red onion and beetroot tart 98
refrigeration 108
regenerative farming 19
reusing 106–19
rhizomes 40
rhubarb 34
rice, cooking 80
rice paper rolls 90–1
roasting 79
robots 38
root vegetables 16, 43, 48
roots 14, 18

salad dressing 83
salsa 93
salting food 110
salty (taste) 52
sautéing 77
saving seeds 11
seasoning 78

seeds 6–13
  as food 7
  banks 8
  coat 10
  development 10
  oils 7
  pods 7
saving seeds 11
seedlings 10, 12–13
transport 6–7
shake it all about butter 118
shipping containers 65
shopping local 63
smell, sense of 54, 121
soda bread 101
soil 14–23
  bacteria 15–16, 19
  formation 15
  horizons 15
  improvement 18
  life 16
  pH 22–3
  testing 22–3
  texture 23
  types 14
sour (taste) 53
spices 78
spicy food 56
spill the beans and share the love 124
spring onions 20
stock, chicken 117
storing food 50
strawberry yogurt pops 104
sugar 52
sugaring food 111
sunlight 32
supermarkets 67
sweet (taste) 52
sycamore seeds 7

table manners 123
taste 52–9

taste a rainbow 59
taste test 58
taste-buds 54
tin opener 109
tinned food 109
tomato salsa 93
tomatoes 49, 122
  seeds 11
  tomato salsa 93
  tomato sauce 86
trees 20

ultra-processed foods 65
umami 53

vegetable families 42–3
vegetable patch 42
vegetables, definition 7

waggle dance 28
wasps 27
water 33
  in food 63, 109
  in soil 18, 23
water butts 33
watering can 41
watering plants 33
weeds 32
wind pollination 27
Wood Wide Web 20
worms 16–17
wraps 99
write a story or poem 124

yogurt 111
  homemade 104
  yogurt pops 104

Acknowledgements

I want to thank my nieces and nephews for keeping me on my toes: Michael the oldest, his brother Daniel and their sister Emily; Cillian and Eva in Cork; Liam in Canada; baby Lila and the others who I may not have met yet.

Thank you to Lola for proofreading and for the meticulous and helpful notes.

Thank you to my sisters and brother and their other halves for always being there.

Thank you to my mother and father for feeding us, not just physically but with knowledge, love and care. Thank you, too, for also having the patience to teach me to cook – and thanks, Dad, for teaching me how to segment an orange.

Thank you to my husband and our beautiful daughter, Della, for the support through late nights, sudden losses and a pandemic. Thank you for the Saturday morning pancakes and the Friday evening chats, the walks in the woods and the scooting on the green.

Thank you all for making life fun. There is probably a part of all of you in the book.

About the author

Michelle Darmody has always loved food – sharing it, cooking it and especially eating it. She was lucky enough to grow up in Cork in Ireland, where she grew lots of vegetables, fruit and flowers in her garden.

Michelle studied art in college but worked in restaurants and cafés in the evenings. She eventually found herself doing more and more of this work.

She travelled the world working in lots of interesting restaurants before coming home to Ireland and opening a cake shop. After running that for 11 years, she decided to focus more on writing about the many ways that food affects the world and studied to be a Doctor in Culinary Arts.

Michelle now writes for a newspaper and helps children to learn about food and the environment. She still loves art and believes that working in food is a way to be creative.